LIVING WITH THE GODS

JACQUELINE DINEEN

ILLUSTRATED BY ROBERT INGPEN
CONSULTANT: PHILIP WILKINSON

DRAGON'S WORLD

CHILDREN'S BOOKS

Dragon's World Ltd
Limpsfield
Surrey RH8 0DY
Great Britain

First published by Dragon's World Ltd, 1995

Text and captions by **Jacqueline Dineen**
based on *A Celebration of Customs & Rituals of the World*
by Robert Ingpen and Philip Wilkinson.

Editor: Diana Briscoe
Designer: Megra Mitchell
Art Director: John Strange
Design Assistants: Victoria Furbisher
and Karen Ferguson
Editorial Director: Pippa Rubinstein

British Library Cataloguing in Publication Data
The catalogue record for this book is available from the British Library.

ISBN 1 85028 304 4

Typeset in Bembo, Garamond and
Opti-Announcement by Dragon's World Ltd
Printed in Italy

Contents

Introduction

The world's religions are all very different, yet there are certain things about them that are similar. In some societies, people worship gods. In others, they revere spirits of nature or of their ancestors. But nearly every culture worships something. Why is that?

How is it that people spread all over the world have developed separate religions, which all aim to communicate with higher beings who can help them to cope with the problems of the world?

Ever since the very first civilizations, religion has been used to explain puzzling things about the world and the things that happen in it. Religion has also bound people together in a system of rituals and ceremonies which give some shape to their lives. Over the centuries, different cultures have developed their own rituals for worship. Some meet in temples, churches or synagogues for formal ceremonies. Others gather in more informal groups.

Some rituals involve music, singing and dancing as a way of calling up the gods. In others, people pray quietly to themselves or with a priest leading the congregation. Some people kneel to pray. Others stand or sit. Yet whatever form the ceremonies and rituals take, their aims are the same: to communicate with the gods in a way that both can understand.

In this book, we look at the ways in which people conduct their worship in different parts of the world. We see how religion has developed since ancient times and how some are no longer followed. By comparing the ways in which people communicate with their gods, we can see that they are very different, and yet in many ways they are the same.

THE RELIGIONS OF *the world take many forms, from societies who worship spirits of nature to religions such as Islam and Christianity, where people worship one god. Buddhists do not worship gods at all, but instead try to find a way to peace and harmony in their lives.*

Religions of the Past

We do not know exactly when people began to worship gods, but we do know that it was at least 30,000 years ago. Since then, people in every corner of the world have developed their own religions, each with its own god or gods to worship.

There have been thousands of gods through the centuries. Some of these are still worshipped today, but many more have long since disappeared. The majority of people in the world today follow one of only a handful of religions such as Christianity, Buddhism or Islam. Yet we know the names of more than 2,500 gods who have been worshipped by someone somewhere at some time in history. There are thousands more whose names have never been recorded. So what happened to these lost gods?

Early peoples looked to their gods to explain all the strange things that happened in the world around them. Only the gods could make the Sun shine, the rain fall, night turn into day. The people of the ancient civilizations worshipped many different gods who were responsible for different aspects of their lives. Although the religion of each civilization was different, we can see similarities between them.

Most ancient religions had a sun god, who was often the most important god since the ancients realized that there could be no life without the Sun. There were gods of war, love, the sea, the sky, hunting, wisdom, the home, the family and the staple crops. Some gods took animal form, while others looked like humans. The gods of each civilization lived in some form of heaven. Belief in an afterlife was very strong among all the

ancient civilizations. There were gods who ruled over the underworld, where the dead went. People consulted their gods before they planted their crops, went on a journey or set out to conquer new lands. Offerings or sacrifices were often made to please the gods and so ensure a successful outcome.

The gods of some ancient civilizations died out with the civilizations themselves. As people learned more about the world, they began to answer questions by scientific reasoning, and felt they did not have to rely on gods quite as before. The gods of other ancient civilizations were overtaken by new religions. For example, Christianity replaced the worship of many different gods in Europe and other parts of the world. Buddhism, which began with the teachings of Buddha in about 500 BC, replaced earlier religions in India and the Far East. One of the oldest surviving religions is Hinduism which began in India in about 1700 BC.

But even though these religions died out, they still helped to shape the world we live in. People still marvel at the temples and pyramids of ancient Egypt, and the architecture and sculpture of ancient Greece has been a model for generations of artists. So how did the religions which inspired these works begin?

IN CHINA, A week before the new year starts, the kitchen god must go up to heaven and report to the Jade Emperor on how the family has behaved during the year. The god is represented by a picture pasted on the wall above the stove. On New Year's Day, a new picture is pasted up to show that the god has returned to his post.

•Egypt•

In the second century BC, the Greeks declared that the seven most magnificent structures in the world should be known as the 'Seven Wonders of the World'. Of these seven ancient wonders, only one has survived. This is the group of three pyramids at Giza near Cairo on the banks of the River Nile in Egypt.

The pyramids were royal tombs. The three at Giza were built between 2550 and 2470 BC for King Khufu, his son Khafre and Khafre's son, Menkaure. Guarding the pyramids is the 73-metre-long Sphinx, with its lion's body and man's head representing Khafre.

Why did the Egyptians bury their kings in such elaborate tombs? The reason lies in their beliefs about gods. The Egyptians worshipped many gods and one of these was the pharaoh himself. They believed that the pharaoh was an earthly representation of the sky god, Horus. When the pharaoh died, he joined the sun god, Ra, and sailed through the heavens in a sacred boat. The shape of the pyramids may represent the rays of the Sun up which the dead king climbed to heaven.

The civilization of ancient Egypt lasted for nearly 3,500 years, and its religion was very complex. When people first began to settle in communities in Egypt, each town had its own gods. Some of these took the form of animals such as cows, monkeys and crocodiles. They were often shown with animal's bodies and human heads. Other gods represented the Sun, the Moon and the stars.

By about 3400 BC, these separate communities had become two kingdoms, known as Upper and Lower Egypt. About 200 years later, Menes, a king of Nekhen in Upper Egypt, conquered Lower Egypt, and united the two kingdoms into one nation. So the gods also had to be united in some way. Some of the lesser gods remained local, while others were merged to make single gods with characteristics from different areas. Gods such

ONE OF THE *massive stone statues found at the Temple of Karnak. The ancient Egyptians spent much of their lives trying to please the gods and provide themselves with a pleasant afterlife.*

as Horus, Ra, the sun god, and Ptah, the god of Memphis, who were worshipped in the great cities, became national gods.

The Egyptians spent their lives trying to please the gods so that they would be accepted in the afterlife. Workers devoted

their energies to building pyramids for the pharaohs, partly because they were ordered to do so, but also to please the pharaoh and, through him, the other gods. Artists were not interested in carrying out work for the living. They concentrated on decorating tombs and temples, which is where most of our knowledge about the Egyptians comes from.

The dead were thought to need their earthly bodies and worldly possessions in the afterlife. Bodies were mummified to preserve them. People were buried with things such as food and pots. The tombs of the pharaohs, their queens and wealthy nobility were also filled with treasures of every sort. The walls of the tombs were painted with scenes from history and everyday life, and the buildings were often guarded by massive sculptures such as the Sphinx, the giant statues of Rameses II which flank the entrance to the Great Temple at Abu Simbel, and the huge statues which

STONES TO BUILD *the pyramids were transported along the River Nile on boats, and then hauled up ramps on sledges. It took about 50,000 people to build the Great Pyramid at Giza – most of them were probably slaves.*

surround the temple of the Theban sun god, Amun, at Karnak.

In 332 BC, Egypt came under first Greek and then later on Roman rule. The ancient gods and temples were still recognized until the end of the second century AD, by which time the civilization had declined and it was easy enough for the Romans to convert the Egyptians to Christianity.

Many of the treasures from the days of the pharaohs were gradually buried under sand, where they lay forgotten until archaeologists began to rediscover them in the nineteenth and twentieth centuries.

•Mesopotamia•

Egypt was one of the most famous and long-lasting of the ancient civilizations, but it was not the first. Between 4000 and 3000 BC, the world's first cities began to appear in the fertile valley between the Tigris and Euphrates rivers in what are now Syria and Iraq. The Sumerians who built these ancient cities invented a system of writing and were the first to use wheeled vehicles. The land where they settled was named Mesopotamia, which means 'the land between two rivers'.

Each city was under the protection of a different god, whose home was the temple complex which dominated the centre of the city. There was often a huge stepped pyramid called a 'ziggurat' in the temple complex. The ziggurat was a solid structure built of brick. At the top was a sanctuary where the god could go when he descended from the heavens. The most famous example is the ziggurat at Ur, which was built in about 2100 BC for the moon god, Nanna.

The Sumerians worshipped more than 2,000 different gods. Each person chose a personal god to worship in addition to the

LEONARD WOOLLEY FOUND *head-dresses like this one in the royal tombs of Ur. The women attendants had dressed in all their finery before committing suicide to follow their mistress into the afterlife.*

main god who protected their city. The people believed that their only purpose in life was to please the gods. They spent as much time as they could praying, and when they had to go away and do other things, they left small statues of themselves to carry on praying for them. Several of these statues have been found – they have huge round eyes which stare out in devotion, and their hands are clasped tightly in prayer.

MUSICIANS PLAYED ON *harps as the funeral procession entered the tomb. Servants led ox-carts, which were filled with offerings for the afterlife.*

In 1922, the British archaeologist, Sir Leonard Woolley, began to excavate the city of Ur. One of his discoveries was a royal burial ground which gives a gruesome insight into Sumerian beliefs about death. Like the Egyptians, the Sumerians believed in an afterlife where worldly possessions were needed. Kings and queens were buried with gold and silver jewellery, head-dresses, musical instruments, pots and ornaments. They were also buried with their courtiers and servants who would presumably continue to serve them in the afterlife. These attendants had followed the body into the tomb, arranged themselves in order of rank and swallowed a cup of poison. The tomb was then sealed up.

THE TEMPLE COMPLEX, *topped by the huge ziggurat, towered over the bustling streets of Ur. This stepped pyramid was built of millions of bricks and its construction was an amazing feat for such an early civilization.*

When Woolley discovered the burial ground, many of the tombs had been plundered, but two remained intact. The skeletons of the men and women were still adorned in the finery they had put on for the occasion. One female attendant had a ribbon from her head-dress in her pocket. Perhaps she had taken it with her to put on in the afterlife. A golden cup lay near each skeleton.

One tomb, known as the Great Death Pit, contained seventy-four skeletons. This was the tomb of King Meskalamdu and dates from about 2500 BC. The king's helmet was in the tomb, where Woolley also found the Royal Standard of Ur. This was a wooden box which was probably the sounding board of a musical instrument. It was decorated with mosaic pictures in shell and lapis lazuli showing life in Sumeria.

·Greece and Rome·

The first civilization in Europe was created by the Minoans on the island of Crete in about 2500 BC. Little is known about the religion of the Minoans, although statues and wall paintings of a snake goddess or priestess were found at Knossos, the palace of the legendary King Minos from whom the Minoans get their name.

The Minoans were replaced by the Mycenaens who built up a civilization on mainland Greece. They were a rich and powerful people, but by 1200 BC, they too had disappeared. Greece then entered a period known as the Dark Ages until about 800 BC, when a new civilization began to develop. This reached its peak in the Classical period which began in the city of Athens in about 500 BC. The Greeks worshipped twelve main gods, plus many minor ones, and the magnificent temples, sculptures and paintings created during the Classical period were dedicated to them. The most famous of all is the Parthenon, a temple to Athena, which stands on the Acropolis in Athens.

All Greek towns and cities had temples where people could go to worship. Each temple was built as a home for the god or goddess that it was dedicated to. Inside, there was a shrine where worshippers left offerings, but the people prayed outside at an altar in front of the temple. If praying was not enough to solve a problem, people could consult an oracle. This was a priestess who spoke on behalf of a particular god. People came from all over Greece to consult the oracle called the 'Pythia' at the Temple of Apollo at Delphi.

Greek religion also inspired the birth of another branch of art – the theatre. The earliest type of theatre was a festival of song and dance in honour of Dionysus, the god of wine. By the Classical period, every large city had its own open-air theatre where plays by writers such as Sophocles and Aristophanes were performed.

When the Romans began to take over the Greek empire in 168 BC, they adopted many Greek ideas. They took Greek works of art to Rome and copied their architecture. They

The twelve most important gods were said to live on Mount Olympus in north-east Greece. They included Zeus, the god of the sky, Apollo, the god of poetry and music, Ares, the god of war, Aphrodite, the goddess of love and beauty, and Athena, the goddess of wisdom and war.

ROMAN TEMPLES WERE *similar to Greek temples in design. An imposing flight of steps led up to the main part of the temple. The triangular section over the entrance was supported by decorative columns. Inside there was usually a statue of the god or goddess and an altar where worshippers could burn incense.*

also adopted Greek gods, simply changing their names to Roman ones. For example, Jupiter was the Roman version of Zeus, Venus was Aphrodite, Neptune was the Roman Poseidon, god of the sea, and Athena became Minerva, goddess of wisdom.

Roman temples were also very similar to the Greek, with a roof supported by columns with carved decorations at the top. Like the Greeks, the Romans left offerings inside the temples, but prayed outside. Roman priests looked for omens before doing anything, and people visited religious officials called 'augurs' who were believed to be able to predict the future. The English word 'augur', as in 'that augurs well for the future', comes from the name for these Roman fortune-tellers.

The Romans continued to worship many gods until Emperor Constantine I made Christianity the official religion of the Roman empire in AD 324. Constantine succeeded a number of emperors who had been worshipped as gods in their own lifetime. They had resented and persecuted Christianity because it threatened their cult. But Constantine realized that Christianity could pull his ailing empire together. He converted to Christianity himself and built many churches including the magnificent Hagia Sofia in Constantinople.

• Scandinavia •

The Vikings who lived in Norway, Sweden and Denmark continued to worship their own gods long after Christianity had spread to other parts of Europe. The Vikings are normally remembered for their warlike behaviour as they plundered their way around Europe, attacking monasteries and stealing their treasures. But when they returned home to Scandinavia, they settled down into a more peaceful lifestyle as farmers who sat around the fire at night, telling stories.

The Vikings believed in many gods and goddesses who lived in the Viking heavens, Asgard. The most important Viking god was Odin, a wise god who understood the magic of 'runes', the Viking method of carving inscriptions in stone or wood. He is often depicted on an eight-legged horse called Sleipnir. Thor, the god of thunder, was a big god with a red beard. When thunder rumbled during a storm, the Vikings said that Thor was riding across the sky in his chariot. Another popular god was Frey, the god of love and marriage. He was also the god of rain and sunshine so he was an important god to turn to throughout the farming year.

The Vikings believed that the Earth, Midgard, was surrounded by a deep ocean full of monsters. Beyond this ocean were giants who wanted to destroy the gods, and a cold, gloomy place called Niflheim. Vikings who died in bed, from illness or old age, went to the miseries of Niflheim. But warrior Vikings who died in battle went to Valhalla, the hall of Odin in Asgard. They would help Odin in his final fight against the giants. Viking chieftains were often buried in a ship which would take them to their new life. One 'grave ship' found at Oseberg in Norway contained two bodies, thought to be a Viking queen and her servant. The bodies were surrounded by food and possessions for the afterlife, including jewellery, kitchen utensils, chests and a carved wagon.

There were three main religious feasts each year, one in the summer, one after the harvest and one in winter. The feasts were celebrated in the family home since the Vikings had only a few temples. A horse was sacrificed, and the gods were asked to bring a successful harvest or victory in battle. Then the horse meat was cooked, and everyone ate their fill, washed down with strong ale. The feasting often went on for two weeks.

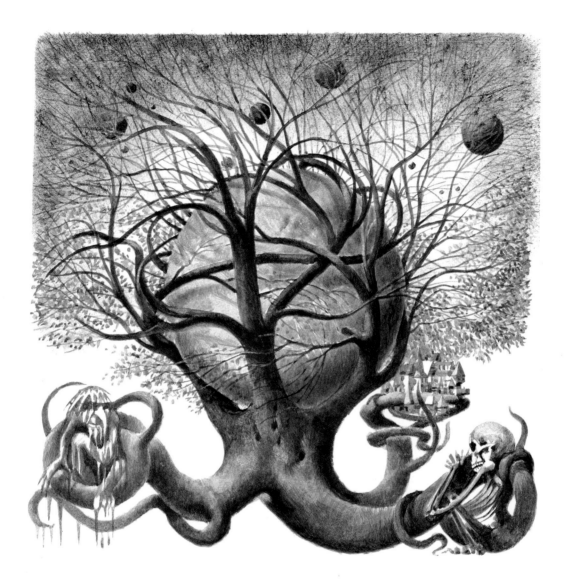

▲ IN NORSE MYTHOLOGY, *Yggdrasil was an evergreen tree with three huge roots. One led to the under world, Niflheim, ruled over by Hel; the second led to Jotunheim, the home of the Frost Giants; and the third led to Asgard, which was the home of the gods. Demons were always attacking the tree, gnawing at its roots, and trying to destroy the link between the worlds. However, the three Norns (or Fates) protected the tree and watered it every day from the three fountains which ran from its base.*

The Vikings took their religious ideas to the lands they conquered, where they were often less than welcome. By the time they attacked the monastery at Lindisfarne off the coast of Scotland in AD 789, for example, Britain was already a Christian country, and the Vikings were looked on as heathen invaders. They did not give up, however, and came close to taking over the whole of England before being defeated by King Alfred the Great at the Battle of Edington. Alfred struck up a deal with the Viking leader, Guthrun. The Vikings were given a stretch of land in the north of England which came to be known as the 'Danelaw', and Guthrun had to promise to convert to Christianity. But stone crosses showing both Christian and Viking gods still stand in many churchyards in northern England as evidence that the two religions once existed side by side.

•Central America•

Civilizations developed in Central America from about 1300 BC and continued to thrive until the Spaniards conquered the last empire, of the Aztecs, in 1521. These civilizations grew up quite separately from those in other parts of the world. In fact, the people had no idea that there was any more to the world until the Spaniards arrived. But each succeeding culture borrowed from earlier ones, so we can trace many similarities between them.

The first great civilization, the Olmecs, grew up in the humid, swampy jungles near the Gulf of Mexico. The Olmecs were artistic people who left behind many sculptures and carvings, including some colossal stone heads depicting Olmec rulers. Archaeologists have also discovered ceremonial centres where the gods were worshipped. These are the earliest of the solid pyramids which continued to be the style of Central American temples.

The next major civilization developed at the city of Teotihuacan. This site in the Valley of Mexico had become an important religious centre from about 1500 BC. People made pilgrimages to a cave there, which was believed to be the birthplace of the Sun and Moon. In the first century AD, a huge temple, the Pyramid of the Sun, was built. A city began to grow up around the temple, and 500 years later, 200,000 people lived there, making it one of the largest cities in the world at that time. Some of the mysteries of Teotihuacan are who built the city and why was it destroyed in AD 750?

The Maya civilization flourished in Guatemala, Honduras and Yucatan between

ARCHAEOLOGISTS HAVE FOUND *huge stone heads like this one, portraying Olmec rulers. They built the first pyramid temples and were skilled artists and sculptors. Because they lived in a region where there was little stone, they often used clay.*

AD 300 and 900. The Maya were the first of the Central American civilizations to invent a system of writing and to work out a calendar. They borrowed ideas from the Olmecs when they built their large cities such as Copan in Honduras. At the centre of their cities stood a pyramid temple, which was built in stepped layers. A long flight of steps led up the side of the temple to the sanctuary at the top. Here, priests and their helpers carried out religious ceremonies and made sacrifices to the gods.

The next civilization to dominate the area after the collapse of the Maya were the Toltecs whose capital city was Tula in Central Mexico, but they had another major centre at Chichen Itza. The last people to take power after the destruction of Tula in about 1150 were the Aztecs. They built the vast city of Tenochtitlan, now under Mexico City, with pyramid temples modelled on those at Tula and Teotihuacan. From here, they built up the mightiest empire of ancient America.

As well as borrowing ideas for temple design, the different peoples seem to have adopted the same gods. For example, one of the principal Aztec gods, Quetzalcoatl, the 'Feathered Serpent', was also worshipped by the Maya, and there are temples dedicated to him in Tula and Teotihuacan.

The Aztecs worshipped many gods and had particularly bloodthirsty methods of pleasing them. Most important was the sun god, Huitzipochtli who, they believed, had sent them to find the site of Tenochtitlan. Huitzipochtli had to be fed with a constant supply of human blood and hearts, otherwise the Sun would fade and the world would end. The Aztecs fought wars not simply to gain new lands, but also to capture prisoners who could then be sacrificed to the gods. Each prisoner was held down on a sacrificial stone at the top of the temple while the priests plunged a knife into his chest and ripped his heart out. The Spanish reported that the priests would sacrifice up to a hundred prisoners in an important ceremony.

THIS IS THE *temple complex from Copan in Honduras, which was built by the Mayans. Priests climbed up the long flights of steps to the temple at the top of the pyramid to worship the god or goddess. They also carried out sacrifices on top of the pyramid, some of which were very bloody.*

Prayers & Worship

The gods of the ancients may have long since disappeared, but many people still feel the need to follow a religion. Religion helps to explain the unknown. Even in an age when science has explained many of the things that happen in the world around us, there are still unanswered questions. How did the world begin? Where does the universe end? What happens to us when we die? Why are we here?

One way of trying to explain the unknown is to believe that there are wiser beings than humans who control the world and everyone in it. People can also draw comfort from their faith in a religion. The belief in a god or gods helps them when they feel they cannot cope with the hardships of life. It comforts people to know that they have someone to turn to.

 People can pray and worship on their own, but most feel the need for some kind of ritual or ceremony where worshippers gather together. They want a structure to follow which sets an example for the way people behave. Most religions expect people to follow certain laws and patterns of behaviour. The need to do this puts a sense of direction into many people's lives.

Why do people pray? Once they have found faith in a god or gods, it is natural that people want to communicate with them, to ask questions or ask for help with problems. Worshippers can build up a special relationship with their gods through regular prayer. In many religions, statues and other images help the worshippers to picture what each god might look like. The images and the teachings of the religion itself concentrate the mind on the gods they are praying to.

In many religions, praying regularly is a law which must be followed by worshippers if they want to be sure of going to paradise or a good life after death. In Islam, people are called to prayer five times a day, when they are expected to go to the mosque if they can. Observing the call to prayer is one of the five important religious duties, known as the 'Five Pillars of Islam'. Christians are expected to go to church regularly, although private prayer is also acceptable.

The way in which prayers are said and the rituals carried out vary greatly from one religion to another. But they all have one thing in common. They bring people together for an occasion that is both formal and familiar, and gives them the feeling that their prayers are being heard.

▲ ROMAN CATHOLICISM
Roman Catholics follow a ritual of confessing their sins to a priest. The idea of the confession and the penance that has to be carried out is to persuade the person not to act in the same way again.

RITUAL AND ACTION

Many religious rituals are concerned with showing people how to act or how to behave. Some rituals are designed to show people how to follow the teachings of the ritual. Others give them guidance on how to behave in their everyday life.

▲▲ BUDDHISM
In some places, it is traditional for Buddhists to free a caged bird at a shrine as a way of showing respect for the freedom of all living creatures.

▲ ISLAM
Muslims learn about the teachings of their religion and the way they are expected to behave by studying their holy book, the Qur'an or Koran.

Positions for Prayer

People of different religions pray to their gods in many different ways. In some religions, worshippers chant loudly. In others, they pray silently or in a low mumble. But whichever way they pray, they are following ritual procedures for communicating with their gods. Sometimes incense is burned or candles are lit to concentrate the person's mind and help put other thoughts out of their heads.

In most religions, there is also a special ritual position for prayer. Putting the hands together stops other movements and fidgeting. Closing the eyes helps people to concentrate and not be distracted by what is going on around them. Kneeling is a position of humility before a more powerful god.

KNEELING
A Muslim kneels, with his head bowed, on a prayer mat which has been placed to face the holy city of Mecca.

HANDS CLASPED
Christians traditionally pray with hands clasped together.

PRAYER BEADS
People of many religions use beads to help them count the number of times a prayer has been said.

LOTUS POSITION
Buddhists may meditate in the lotus position of yoga, cross-legged with each foot on the opposite thigh.

·Fire & Light·

Firelight and candlelight have great significance for many of the world's religions. Christians see candlelight as a symbol of the light that Christ brought into a dark world. This is symbolized by the ceremony of kindling the new fire during the ceremony for the vigil of Easter.

Roman Catholics light candles in church in memory of someone who has died, in thanksgiving, or when they want to make a special

Jews celebrate Chanukah, the Festival of Lights, in December. This commemorates a Jewish victory over the Syrians in 165 BC. The celebrations last for eight days. Candles are placed in an eight-branched candlestick called a 'menorah'. A new candle is lit on each day of the festival until, on the eighth day, all eight are alight. The eight candles are lit because when the temple was retaken after the Syrian invasion, the Jewish soldiers found that a lamp had continued to burn there for eight days even though it only had one day's supply of oil in it.

The Japanese festival of Obon, when the spirits of ancestors are supposed to return to their homes, is held in the middle of the year. Fires, reeds of hemp and coloured lamps are lit to show the family spirits the way home.

Diwali, the Hindu Festival of Lights, is celebrated in October or November, and is in honour of Lakshmi, the goddess of wealth. For four or five days, oil lamps burn in house windows, which are left open to let the goddess in. The streets and temples are also ablaze with lights. This feast is also celebrated by the Sikh community.

FIRES & CANDLES

The flame of a candle is a symbolic show of light which can be used in homes, churches or temples. In traditional religions, firelight is used as a centrepiece for dancing or as an inspiration to meditation.

It may also present a challenge to those who must go through initiation ceremonies such as walking over burning hot coals.

HINDU
In the ceremony of Arti, the priest carries five candles.

JEWISH
The lighting of candles marks the 'Shabat' or Sabbath.

TRADITIONAL
Fire-walkers in Fiji and elsewhere walk barefoot across red-hot coals, but feel hardly any pain.

NATIVE AMERICANS
The Pueblo people would meditate by the fireside on the god of thunder.

Offerings

People have always made offerings or sacrifices to their gods. In the past, people or animals were often killed to please the gods. During the 1960s, about ten human bodies were found in the Tollund Fen in Denmark while excavating for peat. They had been perfectly preserved by the acid in the soil. They were dressed in special clothes, had eaten a special meal – a sort of porridge made from various types of grain – and had all been strangled with a leather thong before being thrown into the bog. It is thought that they had been sacrificed to the god Frey (see page 18) who had had a large temple nearby.

Blood sacrifices are less common these days, although they are still carried out in some remote communities. But people of all religions still make offerings to their gods, often of food or money.

In China, where people worship the spirits of their ancestors, there are three main occasions for making offerings. These are three special festivals in memory of ancestors. The first, Qing Ming, the Festival of Pure Brightness, is the most popular. People visit their ancestors' tombs to tidy them up and leave offerings there. During the second festival, families leave generous offerings at temples and shrines in an attempt to ward off evil spirits and ghosts who might have designs on the spirits of their ancestors. The third festival involves visiting the tombs again, this time to leave offerings of paper clothes and mock paper money to keep the ancestor spirits going in their new life.

An ancient Hindu text states that the gods exist by gifts from below just as people exist by gifts from above. Hindus used to ensure the gods' existence by making blood sacrifices, but today worshippers simply leave food, drink, flowers and coloured powders in front of statues of gods and goddesses in the temples. Hindus should make five offerings each day, but many now carry out this ritual once a day.

The most common type of offering is money which often goes towards maintaining the place of worship or helping people in the community. Christians hand round the collection plate at church services for people to put money into. Among Muslims, one of the 'Five Pillars of Islam' is to make donations to the poor. Buddhist monks are supported by offerings of money, clothing and food from worshippers in their community.

The Yoruba people of Nigeria worship many gods – one of the most popular is Ogun, the god of war and hunting. Every year, a festival is held for Ogun, at which hunting dogs are sacrificed. The festival may be celebrated by whole towns or by individual families. A day is chosen for the feast, and the head of each family must then prepare himself by not cursing, fighting or eating certain foods beforehand. The people gather at the shrine of Ogun for an all-night vigil before the sacrifices are made the next day. Offerings such as snails, pigeons, palm oil and kola nuts are also made.

BUDDHISTS BELIEVE THAT *giving money and food to their monks will help them to a better life when they are born next time.*

▲ SOME OFFERINGS WERE *more bloodthirsty. The Yoruba people of West Africa had a novel way of pleasing the gods and getting rid of their problems at the same time. Every so often, when problems were heaping up on the community, they would make a sacrifice to the gods. First, someone was chosen to be the unfortunate victim. This person, known as the* 'oluwo', *was given everything he wanted until the appointed day arrived. On the day of the sacrifice, the oluwo was disguised with chalk and ashes and marched blindfolded through the village. All the people ran up and touched him to transfer their troubles to him. Then the oluwo's head was chopped off, taking the people's problems away for ever.*

• Religious Processions •

Processions are a part of all religions. They can be happy or solemn occasions. Processions which are a part of a festival often have a carnival atmosphere, with music and singing. Pilgrimages are quieter and more serious. A procession with its of holy relics acts as an advertisement the streets to watch, cheer, give costumes, music and display for the festival. People line money or even join in.

THE HINDU FESTIVAL *of Navaratri is celebrated for ten days in September or October. Images of the goddess Durga are carried through the streets in processions, and people perform plays based on the* Ramayana *epic poem.*

The movement known as the 'Hare Krishna' sect was founded in the United States in 1965. Its proper name is the International Association for Krishna Consciousness, and its rituals are based on Hinduism. The sect is famous for its processions, when its followers walk through the streets chanting the words 'Hare Krishna' which give the movement its popular name.

IN THE MEDIEVAL Christian church, the three days before the Feast of the Ascension were known as the Rogation Days when everybody prayed for the success of the harvest. In monasteries, the monks would process around the fields saying special prayers and blessing the crops.

THE FEAST OF Idu-l-fitr which marks the end of the fast of Ramadan is celebrated throughout the Muslim world. In Nigeria, Muslims have processions and play music in the streets to celebrate.

Dancing for God

Dancing is one of the oldest ways of communicating with the gods. In ancient times, people would carry out ritual dances before important events such as the harvest. They also believed that natural disasters such as the eruption of a volcano or a disastrous flood happened because the gods were angry. Ritual dancing was a way of pleasing the gods and preventing their anger. The steps had special significance. Stamping the feet and beating drums attracted the attention of the gods, while changing direction in a dance symbolized a change such as the end of winter and the beginning of spring.

Although most people in the Western world now regard dancing as a social pastime, ancient ritual dances are still practised in many societies today. The dances are believed to have magic powers which make them a particularly effective way of praying and communicating with gods and spirits. Dancers usually wear colourful costumes and head-dresses, and often paint their faces or wear masks.

The people who live on the Indonesian island of Bali are Hindus. Hindus have thousands of festivals, many of which involve music and dancing. To the Balinese, the goddess Durga is evil. One ritual dance involves Durga dressed in animal skins and a hideous mask. The mask is carved by a master craftsman who must sit up all night in a cemetery to give it its magic powers.

Traditional Muslims frown on music and dancing as a form of worship, but one branch of Islam, the Sufis, regard both as an important part of their rituals. Sufis broke away from the strict laws of Islam in the tenth century, and introduced a more mystical way of life. Sufi worship, particularly in Turkey, Iran, India and Pakistan, includes wild

DANCING, OFTEN ACCOMPANIED *by drumming and other rhythmic music, is used by many traditional religions to please the god or goddess or to call him or her down to earth. The arrival of the spirit is sometimes accompanied by wild and uncontrolled laughter among followers of Voodoo in the Caribbean.*

dancing. The most famous examples are the 'whirling dervishes' of Turkey, who dance feverishly around their master to symbolize the planets going around the Sun.

Sometimes dancers get so carried away that they dance themselves into a frenzy. A strange example of this happened in Aachen in Germany in 1374. People had come from all over Germany to celebrate the midsummer feast of St John the Baptist. Suddenly a group of people began to dance. They leaped in the air, whirled and ran frantically through the streets until they collapsed with exhaustion, frothing at the mouth. More and more people joined in the frenzy until the whole town was leaping and whirling through the streets.

The dancing in Aachen had started for no reason except that people had been gripped by some sort of fervour that made them unable to stop. Some of these manic dancers moved on to other towns and started their wild dancing there, and again everyone joined in. By the early fifteenth century, it was quite usual to see dancing mania in towns all over Europe.

In 1418, several people who were gripped in a dancing frenzy in Strasbourg were taken to the chapel of St Vitus, a little-known fourth-century saint who was thought to be able to cure convulsive diseases. Dancing mania then came to be known as 'St Vitus' Dance', a name which is still used for a convulsive nervous disorder today. But why did it happen?

Several explanations have been put forward by historians and others. One is that the Black Death had ended in 1374, and the people may have danced in this mad way to express their joy and relief. Also, in pre-Christian times, the feast of St John had been a midsummer pagan festival in which dancing played an important part. But none of this really explains the strange frenzy that continued to break out from time to time until the eighteenth century.

Priests & Priestesses

In ancient times, priests and priestesses were very powerful because people believed that they were in contact with the gods or spirits. Their direct line to the gods gave them power. People believed that they could bring about a good harvest or a downpour of rain, heal the sick or punish sinners. People were afraid to anger or offend them, as this could bring down the anger of the gods.

Russian Orthodox Bishop, Romania

P riests and priestesses are still powerful figures in some religions, particularly in the traditional cultures where they are often seen as healers and magicians who are in contact with the spirits. In other religions, the priest is not thought to have such special magic powers, but is a person who has studied the religion deeply, and is seen as a link between the worshippers and the god or gods. He or she passes on the teachings of the religion, leads people in prayer, listens to them when they need help and perhaps hears them confess their sins so that they may be forgiven.

Many of the rites of passage carried out in life are religious, and the ceremonies are conducted by a priest. Regular services of worship in a church, synagogue or temple are also carried out by the local priest. It is not surprising then that in all cultures the priest is looked on with respect and may be helped by money and food from the community.

The priest is often set apart by the clothes he or she wears. These may be rich and elaborate or very plain and simple. Monks and nuns wear plain robes which symbolize the simple life they have chosen. In many Christian churches, the priests wear long flowing robes when conducting a service.

Roman Catholic priests wear a variety of colours, from the plain black of a parish priest to the rich reds of a cardinal. Anglican priests wear white robes, while the robes of Eastern Orthodox priests are red and gold.

Pentecostal Priest, South Pacific

Roman Catholic Cardinal, Italy

Anglican Priest, England

Jews & Muslims

A Jewish rabbi does not wear clothes that set him apart from other worshippers, but all Jewish adult males use some special garments and objects when worshipping in the synagogue. They wear a skullcap and a silk or woollen prayer shawl. Two small black leather boxes containing four texts on slips of parchment are bound to the forehead and the left arm.

Jews celebrate the Sabbath, which begins at sunset on Friday and ends at sunset on Saturday. The word Sabbath comes from the Hebrew 'shabat' meaning 'rest', and this is a day of complete rest when even everyday tasks are forbidden. Some Jews will go to the synagogue for a service on Friday evening, but the main day of worship is Saturday.

Jews face Jerusalem when they pray. The scrolls of the Torah, the Jewish holy book, are kept in the Ark of the Covenant, a type of cupboard which is set in the wall which faces Jerusalem. The people turn towards this wall for their prayers. The rabbi preaches a sermon, and there are prayers which consist of blessings, requests and thanks. The worshippers also sing hymns and psalms.

Islam has no official priests, but all Muslims consider themselves to be part of the community of the faithful, the 'umma'. Some men are trained to become religious leaders and conduct the affairs of the community. At the mosque, the three most important officials are the 'imam' or leader, who leads the prayers, the 'khatib' or preacher, who delivers the sermon, and the 'muezzin', who calls the people to prayer.

Before Muslims begin to pray, they must wash their foreheads, hands and feet. All prayers are in Arabic even if that is not the language of the worshippers. Each service, known as a 'Salat', follows strict rituals which vary from place to place. But a typical Salat in India will begin with the worshippers standing on prayer mats, facing Mecca, and then carrying out a list of rituals known as the 'essentials'. There is a call to prayer and the statement 'worship has begun'.

During the Salat, the worshippers will recite from the Qur'an, pray and make statements or 'takbira', all in a strict order. The positions of prayer are standing, bowing from the waist, sitting, kneeling and the prostration. The full set of rituals or 'list of essentials' is called a 'rak'a'. The morning Salat has two rak'as, the sunset one has three, and the others four each.

Hindus & Buddhists

Hindus are divided into a strict class or 'caste' system. Traditionally, there were four castes. They were the 'Brahmans' or priests, who were the most powerful people in Hindu society. Next came the 'Kshatriyas', the soldiers; third were the 'Vaisyas', the farmers and merchants, and fourth, the 'Sudras', the servants and labourers. Last came the 'Chandalas' or 'Untouchables', who were so low down the social scale that they were not a caste at all. Untouchables could not take part in community rituals and were forbidden to go on certain public roads, enter certain temples or draw water from public wells.

The Hindus explained this system by saying that each person was born into a particular caste which was decided by that person's previous life or 'karma'. So, if you had led a very worthwhile previous life, you could come back as a Brahman, but if you had been wicked, becoming an Untouchable was all you could hope for. The caste system is still an important part of Hindu culture. Boys from the upper castes go through several years of strict religious instruction with a 'guru' or teacher. Today, not all Brahmans are priests, and religious ceremonies can be conducted by members of other castes.

A ceremony conducted by a Brahman priest is usually more elaborate than rituals carried out by members of other castes. A Brahman is still seen to have special knowledge about rituals and sacred prayers. He has to carry out a series of rituals three times a day, pray, make offerings and read from the scriptures. These rituals give him the extra purity of spirit which is needed to communicate with the gods.

Buddhism has no priests and no one sacred text like the Qur'an. The religion's founder, Siddhartha Gautama (563–480 BC), who became known as the 'Enlightened One' or Buddha, did not write anything. He discussed his beliefs with his disciples or followers, who then travelled around, preaching about the new religion. Once a year, during the rainy season, Buddha and his followers gathered together to meditate.

After his death, his followers continued his work and the retreats gradually turned into permanent monasteries. Centuries later, several different Buddhist groups wrote down the first texts about the religion.

•God-kings•

Since the days of the pharaohs of Egypt, some peoples have believed that their king or political leader is a god in human form. The Romans worshipped their emperors as gods after their deaths from the time of Julius Caesar. Caesar was not an emperor, but he became the first sole ruler of Rome and her territories in 46 BC. Caesar's adopted son, Augustus, the first emperor, had a temple built in Caesar's name, calling it Divus Julius, or Julius the Divine. It became the custom to add the word 'divus' to the name of each emperor after his death.

In the east of the empire, shrines were dedicated to Augustus during his lifetime. It became a sign of loyalty to pay homage to the emperor. Emperors who followed Augustus expected the same treatment. It is said that Nero saw himself as the god Apollo.

Meanwhile, Christianity was spreading, and Christians denounced the Romans for worshipping men and idols above God. The emperor saw this as a severe threat to his status and many Christians were killed for their beliefs. The Romans continued to persecute the Christians until the emperor Constantine was converted to Christianity and made it the official religion of the empire in AD 324.

Buddhism spread to Tibet in the seventh century, where it clashed with the local religion, a traditional cult called Bon. Eventually, a new form of Buddhism evolved. This was a mixture of Buddhism and Bon, and came to be known as Lamaism. But followers of the new religion were persecuted by Tibetan rulers, and it was 200 years before they could officially establish themselves. By this time, there were two branches of Lamaists, the Dalai Lamas and the Panchen Lamas, and many other separate Buddhist sects.

The different groups became fierce rivals, and there were also political struggles as military forces tried to gain power in Tibet. This unrest ended in the seventeenth century when Guuhri Khan, chieftain of the fierce Mongol people who had built up a great empire in Asia, gave Tibet to the Dalai Lamas. Their leader, also known as the Dalai Lama, became the political and spiritual ruler of Tibet.

Each leader was chosen by oracles after the death of the previous Dalai Lama. He was regarded as the reincarnation (reborn) of the first Dalai Lama and all-powerful by his people. The fourteenth Dalai Lama ruled Tibet until 1959, when the beginning of Chinese Communist rule in Tibet drove him into exile in India.

Shinto is the national religion of Japan, and its followers worship at shrines all over Japan. One of the gods worshipped until 1947 was the emperor of Japan, who was thought to be a descendant of Amaterasu, the sun goddess. Legend has it that Amaterasu did not like the way the people were behaving in

Japan, and sent her grandson Ningi to rule over them. In about 600 BC, Ningi's great-grandson became the first human emperor, Jimmu Tenno, and after that each emperor was worshipped as a god-king.

The last emperor to have this status was Hirohito who came to the throne in 1926. For the first twenty years of his reign, he was worshipped at shrines up and down the land. However, after Japan had been defeated in World War II, the USA was keen to separate Japanese religion and politics which had made the state very powerful. A constitution drawn up in 1947 took away the emperor's godlike status, and he then ruled as an ordinary monarch.

When Hirohito died in 1989, his official funeral was a massive state occasion witnessed by representatives from 163 countries. But alongside it there was a traditional Shinto ceremony where worshippers showed their devotion to their emperor-god.

Leaving the World

S ome people feel so deeply about their religion that they want to devote their whole lives to it. It is not enough to be a priest or priestess. They want to leave the rest of the world behind them and join a monastery or convent as a monk or a nun.

Monks and nuns give up all their worldly possessions, their jobs and family and friends to live a life which is completely devoted to serving their god or gods. In some cases, monks and nuns lead lives of simple contemplation and prayer.

The first Christian monasteries were founded in the fourth century AD, after the collapse of the Roman Empire. They were very important through the period known as the Dark Ages as they became centres of education where people could learn to read and write – many produced great scholars. The monks also made most of the books. As this was long before the days of printing, the books were copied by hand and decorated with beautiful lettering and pictures.

When people decide to 'leave the world' and become monks or nuns, they enter a monastery or convent as a 'novice'. This is a trial period for them to see if they are making the right decision. They leave their money and possessions behind, and wear the simple habits of the order they are joining. They must obey the rules of the monastery or convent. Some orders of monks and nuns take a vow of silence, for example. This means that they are not allowed to speak except at certain times. The rooms they live in are very simple, and much time is spent in prayer and physical work.

When this trial period is over, the novices take solemn vows of poverty, chastity and obedience and promise to devote the rest of their lives to God. Nuns are symbolically wedded to God, becoming 'brides of Christ'.

IN MEDIEVAL TIMES, *monasteries were centres of learning where monks preserved the arts of reading and writing. Most of the books that were written before about 1300 only survived because they were kept in a monastery library somewhere.*

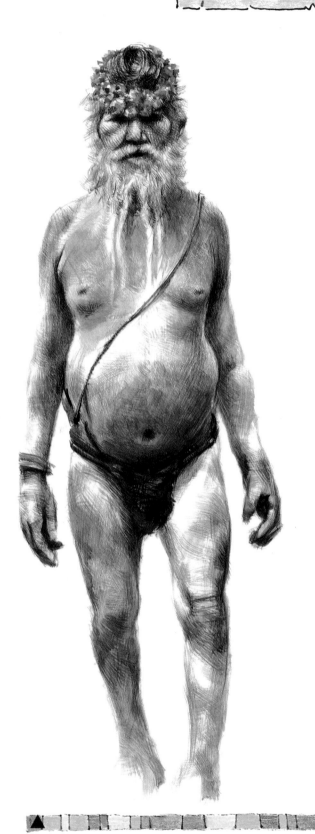

THIS HINDU HOLY *man is an ascetic. These are people who turn their backs on worldly wealth and possessions. Often they leave their homes and their families and wander from place to place trying to find out the meaning of life.*

Buddhist Monks & Nuns

Becoming a Buddhist monk or nun need not be such a final step as it is for a Christian. Many Buddhist boys enter a monastery for only a few months to learn about the religion and the simple life, before settling down to work and marriage. Others become monks for life.

The boy starts by spending seven days at the temple, learning about the ceremony for becoming a monk. On the day before his 'ordination', as this rite is known, his friends bring him the things he will need in his new life. There will be two robes, an umbrella, a pair of slippers, a bowl for food, a lamp, a razor and a begging bowl. The boy's head is shaved, and he puts on a monk's robe. Later that day, the new monks perform a ceremony with the village elders to prepare themselves for their ordination and to steep their minds in their religion.

On the day of the ordination ceremony, the boys are carried to the temple in a procession, attended by two teacher monks. The boys' parents attend the ceremony at the temple. First, each boy pays his respects to his father. There must be five ordained monks at the ceremony, so the boy pays his respects to these monks and asks for permission to be ordained. He is asked some questions to which he must give set answers, and he is then declared a novice. The young novice is then asked some more questions to make sure that he is a suitable person to become a monk. He is told the rules of the monastery, and the ceremony ends with chanting and a blessing. Then there is a feast for the new monks, their relatives and the villagers.

There are fewer nuns than monks, but women have entered monasteries since the time of Buddha. They shave their heads, wear the same robes and follow the same life of meditation and worship as the monks.

·The Navaho People·

The Navaho people migrated from the far north some time between 1200 and 1400, and settled in New Mexico, Arizona and Utah in the United States of America. Traditionally, they were a hunting tribe, but they picked up ideas from their new neighbours, the Pueblo people, and learned to farm the land. This new life did not make them lose their independence and distinctive culture, however, and today they are the largest tribe of native people in North America.

Exactly when and why the Navahos made their trek south is not known because, as time went by, they began to say that they had always lived there. They told stories of their 'Emergence', a long migration from another world to their present world. They marked out an area which was known as 'Dine Bikeyah', or Navaho country. Four sacred mountains formed the boundaries of this land, and within it was the place where, according to their myths, the first Navahos migrated into this world.

Traditional Navaho religion is based on the belief that every part of a person's body and mind must be in perfect harmony, and that this balance can be disturbed by certain types of behaviour, such as coming into contact with ghosts, thinking evil thoughts or showing disrespect to family. Any type of illness is a sign that the balance of the body has been disturbed.

The cure is to conduct a ceremony called a 'chantway'. There are several hundred chantways, each of which retells a special myth or story about the Navahos and their many gods. The ceremony, which lasts between two and fourteen days, must be carried out in a 'hogan', which is

the traditional circular or octagonal lodge.

A type of 'shaman' or priest known as a 'hand trembler' decides which chantway should be used for the person's illness, and a singer is called to perform it. Prayer wands are set outside the hogan to call the gods to the ceremony, and the singer begins the chant, which must be performed with no errors. At certain points during the chant, coloured paintings illustrating the story are laid out in the sand on the floor. The sick person is seated in the middle of these pictures so that the gods shown in them can work on the cure. Everyone present at the ceremony is blessed at the same time.

Traditional Religions

Traditional religions survive in many parts of the world, particularly in Africa, North and South America, Australia and parts of Asia. The beliefs and traditions of these religions have been passed down by word of mouth for centuries.

In traditional religions, people worship or fear gods and spirits which seem to govern the environment they live in. Some traditional cultures believe that there are good and bad spirits in nature. In Zaire in Africa, monkeys are thought to have special powers. In traditional North American societies, beavers have this privilege, while people in the islands of the southern Pacific worship fish. In harsh environments such as the Arctic lands, where people have to survive extremes of climate, they often worship gods of thunder, the sun or the sea.

Ancestor spirits are an important part of many traditional religions. In some cultures, people worship a certain object such as an empty chair or a totem pole which is said to represent the ancestor spirits.

Life is governed by ritual for the people of many traditional cultures because there are good and bad spirits everywhere. The good spirits have to be kept happy and the bad ones have to be kept at bay. A person can be harmed or threatened by the spirits at any time. If someone feels that evil spirits are at work, perhaps because of illness or bad luck of some kind, he or she calls the 'shaman' or priest who conducts a ceremony to get rid of the bad influences. During this ceremony, the shaman's own spirit is freed from his body and goes in search of the evil spirit to tell it to leave its victim alone.

Sacrifices are still made in some traditional cultures. There may be a need to soothe the

PAPUA NEW GUINEA
When someone wears this clay 'tamato' or spirit mask, he becomes the spirit it represents.

PUEBLO PEOPLE, USA
On this figure which represents a kachina spirit, the eyes are shown as rain clouds and the eyelashes as rain.

NEW ZEALAND
This wooden carving represents the Maori god Tangaroa. The god was said to enter the wood and speak through the voice of the priest.

ruffled feelings of the gods or calm their anger. The people may want to give thanks for a good harvest or the arrival of the rains. In Africa, a sheep, a hen or a bull might be sacrificed, while the Ainu people of Japan would sacrifice a bear.

The shaman often wears a mask to help him imitate the spirit he is calling on and a costume which disguises his body. The mask, music, dancing and rituals make people believe that the shaman has communicated with the spirit and brought it into the midst of the people. Only a very few people know how to make the masks or perform the music and dances, and so the ceremonies seem very mysterious and magical to the onlookers. The shaman is set apart as a person with very special powers.

THIS MASK WAS *worn by a member of the secret society of the Igbo people of Nigeria.*

The rules and rituals surrounding the making of these objects can be as complex as the religious ceremonies themselves. One of the simpler ceremonies takes place on the islands of the New Hebrides in the Pacific Ocean, where one of the most important ritual objects is the 'slit gong' or drum which is used to accompany various dances. A man who commissions one of these beautifully carved drums, will give a feast when the instrument is set up on the dancing ground.

A more complex ceremony was held on

The ceremonies of traditional religions are performed using ritual masks, clothes, musical instruments, figures and other objects that are often beautifully painted or carved with a variety of intricate designs.

THE MASK HOUSE

The length of time it took to build the mask house and to make the masks shows how important this ritual was. No one was allowed to see the work while it was going on, and the designs were a closely guarded secret. This made the impact even greater when the men emerged wearing the tall, spectacular masks for the procession along the coast.

had different designs, but they were all the same style, tall and oval with abstract patterns and shapes painted in pastel shades on a grey background.

It could take months or even years to make the masks. When they were finished, a clan member put on the mask, and the rest of the clan gathered around him for a procession down the coast.

Afterwards, everyone celebrated with a feast. Sometimes there was an initiation ceremony for young people at the same time. Then the masks were taken to a special courtyard where they were formally thanked for taking part in the festival and destroyed by fire. This long ceremony helped the people make contact with the spirits and brought good health and successful harvests.

the coasts of southern Papua New Guinea. This ceremony normally took place when a run of bad luck, such as several bad harvests or unexpected deaths, had hit the community.

First, a special mask house was built. This was a solid structure made of logs with a thatched roof, so it took a long time to build. When the building had been completed, the men of each clan gathered in the house to begin the masks. Each clan made and painted a mask which represented a spirit who was particularly important to them. The masks

Places to Pray

Ever since people began to worship gods, they have found or built special places for religious rituals. Before the early civilizations began to build temples, people chose natural places for worship. These places then became sacred. Mountains were a favourite choice because people from many cultures believe that the gods live in the heavens above the Earth. So climbing a mountain brings people closer to the gods. Mountain tops are also remote, secret places which are not easily reached.

A particularly noticeable landmark could also become a sacred place. This might be a large rock such as Ayers Rock in Australia which is 335 metres high and ten kilometres in circumference, making it the world's largest single block of rock.

Caves were probably some of the earliest sacred places. Dramatic pictures of animals and people have been found on the walls of caves, some of them dating back 30,000 years. The most famous examples are pictures painted 15,000 years ago in caves at Lascaux in south-west France. Cave paintings show animals such as bison which would have been the prey of hunters at the time.

The interesting thing is the position of the paintings. They are tucked away in the darkest corners of the caves, and in many cases would have been difficult to reach. This suggests that they were were part of some sort of religious ritual, perhaps to bring luck in the hunt.

Seas and rivers are also sacred to some cultures. People have always been in awe of the power of the sea, believing that violent storms and lashing waves were caused by gods of the sea such as the ancient Greek Poseidon, or Neptune, the Roman god. Sacrifices were made to the gods of the sea in an attempt to tame their temper, particularly before a voyage. People who make their living from the sea, such as fishermen, have always had a variety of customs and rituals to ensure a safe voyage and a good catch.

Some rivers are also thought to be sacred. Hindus regard all rivers as sacred but the Ganges is particularly holy. The Ganges rises in the Himalayan mountains and flows

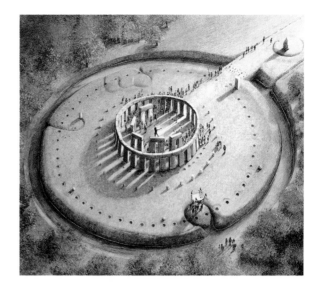

through India and Bangladesh to the Bay of Bengal. Hindus believe that they can wash away their sins by bathing in its waters.

Stonehenge on Salisbury Plain in England is a ring of massive 'sarsens', or standing stones, with horizontal lintel stones on top. Work on Stonehenge began in about 3000 BC, and it was added to and rebuilt many times over the next 1,500 years. The stones had to be brought to the site, cut to shape and then hauled into position without any equipment apart from simple tools, ropes and levers. This makes the building a great feat of engineering. But what was its purpose?

The number of burial mounds around Stonehenge show that it was a very important sacred place at the time. The position of the stones gives a clue about its ritual purpose. They are placed in such a way that on Midsummer Day, someone standing at the centre of Stonehenge can see the Sun passing directly over a stone outside the ring known as the Heel Stone.

Midsummer Day was clearly important to the people who built Stonehenge. People probably gathered there for a midsummer festival to worship the Sun, and give thanks for its return after the long dark days of winter. When the Romans added this part of Britain to their empire in AD 43, the Celts were still using Stonehenge for Sun-worship.

Churches, Mosques, Pagodas...

Most sacred places within a religion have a typical shape and design, and there is usually a focus of attention inside. This may be an image of the god or another symbol.

Christian churches are laid out in the shape of a cross. The altar at the end of the long nave is the focus of attention. People sit in rows facing the altar, and the priest conducts some of the prayers from there. Near the altar, there is a 'pulpit' where the priest preaches the sermon, and a 'lectern' with a Bible for reading the lessons. When people come into church, they face the altar and say a short prayer. Roman Catholics and some other Christians make the sign of the cross as they enter.

A Muslim mosque has a dome and a 'minaret' or tower from which the call to prayer is given. Muslims must wash and take off their shoes as they enter the mosque, so there is a fountain or some other source of water outside the main door. Inside the mosque, the focal point is the 'mihrab' or prayer niche, which shows the direction of Mecca. As worshippers go into the mosque, they find a place where they can face the mihrab. Nearby is the 'minbar', a type of pulpit where the khatib preaches the sermon.

Hindu temples have a porch or canopy outside the main door, where worshippers must remove their shoes. Inside the temple is a sanctuary containing the image of the god or goddess the temple is dedicated to. This is the focal point for worship and offerings.

In a Jewish synagogue, the men sit in the main part of the building, facing the ark where the Torah scrolls are kept. The women usually sit in a ladies' gallery. Beneath the Ark of the Covenant, which is set in the wall facing Jerusalem, is the pulpit on a raised platform. In front of that is another platform from which the Torah scrolls are read.

▲ ISLAM

The muezzin calls the faithful to prayer from the minaret or tower of the mosque. Inside there is a mihrab or prayer niche which shows the people the direction of Mecca. They find a place in the large prayer hall and position their prayer mats so that they can face Mecca when they pray.

FOCUSES FOR RITUAL

Religious buildings are specially designed for the types of ritual that will be carried out in them. Muslim mosques have a large carpeted prayer hall where worshippers can find a place to kneel or sit on the floor. Christians and Jews sit on rows of seats for part of the service. All worshippers face a focal point, and the priests and other participants in the service usually speak from somewhere near this point so that everyone can see what is going on.

▲ BUDDHISM

A pagoda is one type of Buddhist shrine or temple. The shrine is often dominated by an image of the Buddha. Buddhists do not worship the Buddha, but follow his teachings. Part of the Buddhist ritual involves making offerings, paying respect to the Buddha, meditating and chanting verses.

▲ CHRISTIANITY

The altar or 'Lord's table' is the focus in a Christian church. The central ritual of 'Eucharist' or 'Holy Communion' takes place there. The priest blesses bread and wine, in memory of Christ's last meal.

· Pilgrimage ·

Pilgrimage plays an important part in many faiths. A pilgrimage is a journey to a sacred place, and people have been making these journeys for hundreds of years.

A pilgrimage to Mecca is one of the Five Pillars of Islam. All Muslims are expected to make the pilgrimage at least once. It was also on a pilgrimage to Mount Hira that the prophet Muhammad saw the Archangel Gabriel and learned about the new religion.

▲ ISLAM
All Muslims hope to visit Mecca at least once in their lives, wherever they may live in the world. Today, about a million people flock into Mecca for the annual pilgrimage. Before entering the sacred part of the city, the men put on an 'ihram', the traditional dress of the pilgrim. This is a white seamless garment which is worn so that one shoulder is bare. When the pilgrims enter Mecca, they make for the Kaaba in the courtyard of the Great Mosque. This is a stone cube which is said to have been built by Abraham at God's command. The pilgrims must go round the Kaaba seven times, trotting for three circuits and walking for four. Then they perform a Salat and drink from the sacred well, Zamzam. They are then ready to begin the ceremonies which they must complete during the pilgrimage.*

▲ TIBETAN BUDDHISM
One of the most sacred places for the Tibetan Buddhist is the monastery of the Jokhang. Like other Buddhist shrines, the monastery was closed during the period when Chinese Communists took over Tibet. It reopened in 1979, and pilgrims began to visit it again. An important image in the monastery is that

During the Middle Ages, the roads were thronged with Christian pilgrims making their way to the Church of the Holy Sepulchre in Jerusalem, St Peter's in Rome, St James of Compostela in Spain, and other holy places. Christians still make pilgrimages to the healing centre at Lourdes in France, where a miller's daughter, Bernadette Soubirous, had visions of the Virgin Mary in 1858, to Fatima in Portugal and other shrines around the world.

of Chenrezi, a spirit who the Buddhists believe was represented by the first of the Dalai Lamas, the spiritual leaders of the Tibetan Buddhists. Pilgrims make offerings of grain at the monastery, and pins are stuck into the image of a three-eyed protective god. This ritual is supposed to sharpen the minds of the pilgrims.

▲ CHRISTIANITY
One of the most remarkable Christian pilgrimages is the Corpus Christi journey to Qoyllur Riti in Peru. The pilgrims have to make a dangerous climb up a sheer glacier near the city of Cuzco, to commemorate the time when Christ is said to have appeared there in 1780. However, Cuzco was the capital city of the Incas, and it is likely that a

similar ritual was carried out in pre-Christian times. A cross is set up on the ice, prayers are said and candles are lit. The mountain is supposed to be a home to the spirits of sinners, but the pilgrims, many of whom are young men known as 'ukukus' or bears, are supposed to be strengthened by their journey, and therefore able to ward off the evil around them.

·To the Ganges and Amritsar·

Hindus make many pilgrimages. On every day of the year, a pilgrimage takes place somewhere in India. Some pilgrimages are short journeys to local sites, while other sites are visited by worshippers from all over India. People make pilgrimages for a variety of reasons.

They may go because they are ill and want to be cured, or because they want to make offerings to their ancestors, or because they feel they have sinned and want forgiveness. Sometimes they feel they need some good luck or help with a new project, and so they make a pilgrimage to ask for this. Local sites all offer different benefits to the pilgrims, and they have a great variety to choose from. Each site has guides and priests who welcome the pilgrims and take them on a conducted tour, explaining the ceremonies that are carried out there and showing them the temples and other features of the site.

Millions of Hindus make a pilgrimage to the holy city of Varanasi to wash away their sins in the River Ganges. Varanasi is one of the oldest cities in India. Its buildings, which include 1,500 temples, come right down to the water's edge, where there are five kilometres of steps known as 'ghats' where pilgrims can bathe. There are also 'burning ghats' where the dead can be cremated and their ashes scattered over the sacred water.

The most important shrine for Sikh worshippers is the Golden Temple which is at Amritsar in the state of Punjab in India. Sikhism was founded in the sixteenth century by Guru Nanak (1469–1539) who was born a Hindu. As a young man, he was dissatisfied with his life and began wandering around India in search of truth and wisdom. One day, when he was meditating in a forest, he had a vision which told him 'There is no Muslim and there is no Hindu.' Nanak then began to preach about Sikhism, which some people see as a combination of the two older faiths, but the Sikhs themselves say was a new religion.

Nine gurus succeeded Nanak, but after the death of the last one, Guru Gobind Singh in 1708, it was decided that the holy book of the Sikhs, the 'Granth Sahib', should be the only teacher of the religion, and any Sikh could conduct religious ceremonies. The Sikh place of worship is called a 'gurdwara', and most ceremonies revolve around readings from the 'Guru Granth Sahib', as it came to be called.

• Muslim Shi'ite Shrines •

The prophet Muhammad taught his followers that they were joining one community in their new religion. Even so, not long after his death, differences of opinion began to arise, and various groups of Muslims broke away.

The two main groups in Muslim religion today are the Sunni, who make up the majority of worshippers, and the Shi'ites, who live mainly in Iran, although there are also some followers in India.

The main reason for the division was a dispute over leadership after Muhammad's death. The leadership of Islam was taken on by a caliph or deputy to Muhammad who ruled over the Muslims in every way except as a prophet. The majority group, who later became the Sunni, believed that the caliphs should be drawn from among Muhammad's friends, beginning with Abu Bakhr, and the Sunni have followed this line of succession ever since. The Shi'ites believe that the prophet's true successors were his family and therefore follow a line of leadership from Muhammad's son-in-law Ali.

Another point of dispute was the teaching of Islam. The Sunni maintained that the Qur'an should be the basis for the religion, whereas the Shi'ites believe that there is always one imam

or leader who is a representative of God on Earth and whose word is law. All members of the Shi'ite faith must submit to the authority of this leader.

In the ninth century AD, a small sect of Shi'ites known as the Ismaili was formed in India. Once again, a leadership dispute was the cause. The Shi'ites had made Musa, a descendant of Ali, the seventh Imam in AD 765. However, the Ismaili believed that the rightful leader should have been his elder brother, Ismael, who had died as a child. Today, the Aga Khan is the Imam of the Ismaili sect, said by his people to be God's representative on Earth.

•Jerusalem•

Of all the holy cities in the world, Jerusalem is the best known, because it has a special importance for three major religions – for the Jews, the Christians and the Muslims.

Jerusalem has a complicated and often unhappy history. The city was conquered by King David in 1005 BC, and later became the capital of Judaea. David's son, Solomon, built the first temple there in 969 BC, but this was destroyed with the rest of the city by King Nebuchadnezzar of Babylon in 586 BC. Many Jews were forced to live as exiles in Babylon until 538 BC, when Babylon was conquered by the Persians, and the Jewish exiles were allowed to return to their city.

Jerusalem was occupied by Alexander the Great in the fourth century BC, and then by the Romans in 63 BC. Jesus was put to death

Through the ages, people of different faiths have made pilgrimages to Jerusalem. During the Middle Ages it was an important place for Christian pilgrims who would make long journeys there on foot. The Mappa Mundi, a medieval map dating from about 1290, marks Jerusalem as the centre of the world, with pilgrims' routes leading to it from all over Europe and the Middle East. At the top of the map, the blessed are shown going up to heaven, and at the bottom sinners are descending into hell.

WAILING WALL
Jews gather at the 'Western Wall' or the 'Wailing Wall', the only part of the temple still standing today, to mourn its destruction and the exile of the Jewish people.

HOLY SEPULCHRE
Christian pilgrims make for the church of the Holy Sepulchre, built on the site of Christ's tomb. The church is shared by Orthodox, Roman Catholic, Armenian, Syrian and Coptic (Egyptian) branches of the religion.

DOME OF THE ROCK
The mosque called the Dome of the Rock is built on the site where Abraham is said to have prepared his son Isaac for sacrifice and also over the rock from which the prophet Muhammad is believed to have ascended into heaven.

during the reign of the fifth Roman ruler, Pontius Pilate. For a while, Jerusalem was the home of both the Jewish and the new Christian faith, until in AD 70, the Romans destroyed the city and the second temple, and many Jews were forced to flee.

Jerusalem was dominated by the Romans and then by the Byzantine Empire until AD 640, when it was captured by the Arabs under the leadership of the second Muslim caliph, Umar. Just over sixty years later, the mosque called the Dome of the Rock was built.

The city was recaptured by the Crusaders, an army of Western Christians who set out in 1095 to recover the holy places of Palestine. A new state called the Kingdom of Jerusalem was created in 1099, but the victory was short-lived. In 1187, the city was recaptured by the Muslim leader, Saladin, and so the conflict surrounding it continued....

·Shinto Shrines·

The name 'Shinto' describes a variety of Japanese religions including magic, folklore and ancestor worship. The word was put together in the sixth century AD to distinguish traditional Japanese religion from Buddhism and Confucianism which had arrived from abroad. It comes from the Chinese 'Shen-tao', the 'tao' or way of the 'shen' or spirits.

Followers of Shinto worship many heavenly gods as well as the spirits of ancestors, heroes or emperors and spirits of nature such as trees, mountains, rocks and water. Because Shinto is such a varied religion, it has no set scriptures, apart from some ancient documents giving legends, early history and the origins of the gods. Prayers and rituals praise the gods or, if necessary, calm them down.

The traditional form of worship is Shrine Shinto. In prehistoric times, people worshipped trees, mountains, rivers and other natural things by praying to the objects themselves. Gradually, they began to build shrines to their gods or objects of worship. Today, there are about 110,000 shrines in Japan. Some are no more than simple shelters or small halls. Others are large, elaborate structures, like the Grand Shrine of Ise on the peninsula of Nagoya, which is dedicated to the sun goddess Amaterasu. The buildings are in a sacred enclosure surrounded by an inner and an outer fence. The shrine has been rebuilt every twenty years since the seventh century.

Shinto became the state religion of Japan during the reign of Emperor Meiji, who came to the throne in 1868. Meiji wanted to separate Shinto from Buddhism, which had many followers, and to make all the people loyal to the national religion and emperor worship. All Shinto shrines were brought under government control, and those linked to emperor worship were looked on with particular favour, while many Buddhist temples were closed down. But Buddhism was a powerful religion, and though it suffered at first, it gradually regained many of its followers.

In 1882, the Meiji government recognized three religions in Japan: Shinto, Buddhism and Christianity. However, all Japanese of whatever religion had to take part in rituals at State Shinto shrines. They had to declare a belief that the emperors were gods in human form, and that the Japanese people were a superior race, descended from the gods.

The government used these religious rules to establish complete political and military control over the people. This situation continued until 1945, when the Japanese government was ordered to put an end to State Shinto and emperor worship at the end of World War II. Today, politics and religion are separate and shrines are kept going by public contributions.

· Islands of the Pacific ·

Around the Pacific lies a belt of volcanic islands forming part of the 'ring of fire'. Over half of all the world's volcanoes are in this ring. The islands were formed by magma from erupting underwater volcanoes which built up over thousands of years. Many islands remain unstable, with volcanoes that could explode at

People began to arrive on these islands about 5,000 years ago. They had set off, probably from China, in large canoes, and the same group of people moved from one island to the next, so keeping one language and culture. Some settled on Fiji, Samoa and Tonga. Others paddled east to Easter Island or north to Hawaii, which consists of twenty separate islands. The islands which lie in a triangle between Hawaii, Easter Island and New Zealand came to be known as Polynesia.

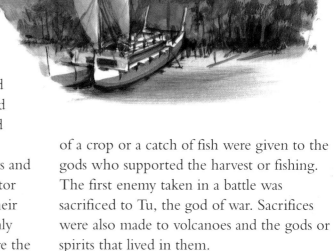

The Polynesians lived in a world which was full of gods and spirits. They believed that the universe was created by the great god Tangaroa, that the earth and sky produced many lesser gods, and that they in turn had produced human beings. These lesser gods presided over different aspects of everyday life and could be called upon for help.

There were also all manner of demons and ghosts to contend with. But noble ancestor spirits were always standing by to help their descendants to prosper on Earth. The only people with a direct line to the gods were the tribal chiefs, who were once believed to be gods themselves, and the priests who were thought to have special knowledge of secret rites and rituals.

The 'tohunga' or priests called up the gods and ancestor spirits with sacred chants at a shrine, or at a special gathering place called a 'marae'. The gods were honoured with relevant offerings. For example, the first fruits of a crop or a catch of fish were given to the gods who supported the harvest or fishing. The first enemy taken in a battle was sacrificed to Tu, the god of war. Sacrifices were also made to volcanoes and the gods or spirits that lived in them.

Polynesian traditions began to disappear when Europeans colonized the islands. Sacred places and ancient beliefs were abandoned as missionaries arrived and converted whole islands to Christianity. Hawaii was annexed by the USA in 1893 and became the fiftieth American state in 1959. However, attempts are being made to bring back some of the traditional Polynesian culture to the islands.

Visions & Penance

Throughout history, people of all religions have seen visions which have made their faith even stronger. Muhammad's vision of the angel Gabriel marked the start of Islam. The grotto near Lourdes in France where St Bernadette said that she had eighteen visions of the Virgin Mary in 1858 is still a place where sick people are taken in the hope of a miraculous cure.

Many North American peoples have a ritual known as a 'vision quest', during which people go out looking for a vision from a guiding spirit. Traditionally, no important event can take place without calling up a vision. The vision quest is used to heal the sick, prepare warriors for battle, ask favours from the gods and give thanks to them in person. All young men are expected to take part in the vision quest. The results settle a man's role and status in his tribe. If he does not see a vision during the ritual, he is barred from certain roles and is not allowed to take a full part in the life of the tribe. If he is successful, however, he can take his place in hunting parties and as a warrior, and can help with religious ceremonies.

The young man must perform five rituals in his quest for a vision. First, he leaves the tribes for a short period of fasting. When this is over, he takes a steam bath to banish all worldly thoughts. He then climbs to the highest hill in the area where he strips to his moccasins and breeches. He must now stand there without moving for several days. But the worst is yet to come. He has to cut off his little finger or strips of flesh from his arm as offerings for the gods. This gesture shows that he is sincere in his wish for a vision.

The young man's vision must include an animal spirit, some sort of promise for the tribe and a token as proof. Members of the tribe who continue to see visions after the original quest qualify for extra duties, such as healing. The shaman meets his guardian spirits on a vision quest and can then call them up at will during rituals in the lodge. The spirits tell him of their presence by tapping the walls or shaking the lodge. The shaman then puts his requests to them.

Hermits

Some people choose to get away from everyone and live alone so that they can meditate and live a more contemplative life. The word 'hermit' is often used to describe anyone who lives on their own, cut off from other people, but it originally meant an early Christian recluse.

Before Christianity had become an established religion, Christians faced much persecution from the Roman emperors and followers of other pagan religions. But when the Roman empire collapsed, Christianity spread among the independent states which began to rise up. Kings such as the powerful Charlemagne of the Franks extended the numbers of Christians among their subjects, making themselves more powerful at the same time. Many of the new Christians were from among the so-called 'barbarian' peoples who took over Europe after the fall of the Roman empire. Most of them could not read or write and as there were no formal guidelines about the religion, people began to form their own movements, tailoring their beliefs to suit themselves.

This state of affairs led to disputes among Christians and forced the Church to establish a formal statement of beliefs and make certain writings sacred. Meanwhile, many men who wanted to protect the message of Christianity withdrew from the world and lived as hermits in deserts and other isolated places around the Mediterranean. The way of life chosen by the hermits paved the way for the establishment of monasteries, which in turn helped the development of Christianity because they were almost the only centres of learning in western Europe during the Dark Ages.

Monasteries had many functions at this time. They formed centres of religion or education and places where the sick and poor could go for help. They also provided places where people could live in an organized society, but could lead the type of Christian life they wanted, away from the divisions and disputes in the world outside.

Meditation & Rituals

Meditation has formed a part of many religions, particularly Eastern ones, for centuries. Meditation involves concentrating on an object, a word or a thought with the aim of clearing the mind and achieving inner peace.

In its simplest form, meditation is a way of relaxing the body and mind by banishing stressful thoughts. With practice, people can achieve a trance-like state when they feel at one with everything in the universe. To the Christian mystic, this means feeling at one with God, while Buddhists feel that they have experienced Nirvana.

The rituals of meditation involve shutting out all outside sounds, so most people find it easier to meditate in a place that is quiet and remote from the hustle and bustle of everyday life. When a person has managed to clear their mind of any thoughts or distractions, he or she focuses on something, which may be an object such as a flower or the flame of a candle, a word or a more abstract thought. The person concentrates on this one thought for a length of time without allowing anything else to intrude. This is called the 'stage of meditation'. A sustained period of meditation, when the person reaches a trance-like state, is called 'contemplation' or 'mystical experience'.

CONTEMPLATION ▶

Many religions have devised rituals to help people reach the trance-like state. People who practise yoga or a martial art such as Tai Chi, or who tap gently on a drum or chant softly to themselves, are using ritual to concentrate their minds.

◀ RETREAT TO THE HILLS

Isolated hilltops, near to the heavens and away from the hustle and bustle of everyday life, are traditional places to meditate. Hills and mountains have always had a special significance in religion. Climbing a mountain so that you are far above the world puts everything into perspective and makes everyday problems seem trivial. And, because the terrain is difficult to tackle, mountains are unlikely to be crowded with other people. So those wishing to meditate have peace and quiet to help them banish stressful or unpleasant thoughts from their minds.

Yom Kippur

People often want to ask forgiveness of their gods, and to do something to prove their faith or make amends for wrong-doing. Confession and fasting are methods used in some religions. Roman Catholic Christians confess their sins to the priest at regular intervals. Many religions have periods of fasting. The Jewish festival of Yom Kippur, the Day of Atonement, is a twenty-five hour ritual of confession, prayer and fasting when everyone asks for their sins to be forgiven before starting the new year.

Rosh Hashanah, or New Year, is one of the two most sacred holy days in the Jewish calendar. It is celebrated in September or October and marks the start of a period of penitence which ends with Yom Kippur, the other most sacred day.

Yom Kippur begins at dusk and lasts till nightfall on the following day. No one is allowed to eat or drink anything during this period, and leather shoes may not be worn because they are symbols of comfort.

Most of the day is spent in the synagogue, praying, fasting and confessing sins.

The Jews believe that God forgives people who truly repent and are sorry for their sins, but that they must try to win his forgiveness and not take it for granted. The twenty-five hour ritual of Yom Kippur is seen as a way of making amends to God and showing that worshippers realize what they have done wrong. Just before sunset on the first day, the whole congregation chants the 'Kol Nidre', in which they ask God to forgive them for breaking promises and not doing things they said they would. Then candles are lit, and families ask each other for forgiveness. Fasting ends at sunset on the second day, and all the members of a family gather together for a celebration meal at home.

Ramadan

The fourth duty in the Five Pillars of Islam is to fast during the month of Ramadan, the ninth month in the Islamic calendar. For thirty days, all Muslims over the age of twelve must not eat or drink anything during the hours between sunrise and sunset, but the restrictions are lifted between sunset and sunrise.

The fast commemorates the time when Muhammad was visited by the angel Gabriel, but it is also linked to the Muslim victory in a battle at Badr during Ramadan in AD 624. Part of the ritual is that Muslims must read one-thirtieth of the Qur'an on each night of the fast. The text of the Qur'an has been divided into thirty sections for this purpose.

Details about the fast are laid down in two verses in the Qur'an. The first verse states that everyone must keep the fast during Ramadan. Anyone who is sick or on a journey may break the fast for that length of time, but must make the days up later. The second verse says 'You are permitted during the night of the fast to ... eat and drink until so much of the dawn appears that a white thread can be distinguished from a black one. Then keep the fast completely until night....'

Muslims are encouraged to eat at the last moment before sunrise and break their fast as soon as possible at night. Just after sunset, a call is given from the minarets of the mosques and the people can then eat a special evening meal called 'iftar'.

As soon as the new moon appears at the end of Ramadan, there is great joy and feasting after the month of hardship. For three days, people celebrate Idu-l-fitr, the festival of fast-breaking. Soon after sunrise on the day after Ramadan, everyone dresses in new or special clothes and the men go to the mosque for prayers. Families and friends visit one another and exchange presents during the festival. Cakes or sweets are favourite gifts. Many Muslims also visit family graves at this time to pray and also offer food and money to the poor.

•Hindu and Buddhist Atonement•

Fasting is a part of many Hindu festivals. Festivals may be local, regional or celebrated by everyone in India, and there are hundreds of different ones. Some are dedicated to the many Hindu gods and goddesses, ancestors and spirits, while others celebrate the seasons or the phases of the moon, or honour snakes, buffaloes, rivers, mountains, plants and other things from the natural world.

BUDDHIST ATONEMENT

Tibetan Buddhists have a ritual called 'Nyungne', which is a period of atonement. They are not allowed to work or have conversations and must go without food and drink for some of the time. There is silence in the temple until the end of the four-day ritual, and children are not allowed in because they would be too noisy.

People are not forced to observe Nyungne, but Buddhists believe that it brings them merit. This is important to Buddhists, because the more merit they can build up to offset the sins committed in life, the better they will be when they are reborn in the next life.

In the Hindu calendar, every month is divided into a light half beginning with the new moon, and a dark half when the moon wanes and disappears. The thirteenth day in the dark half of every month is dedicated to Shiva, the Lord of Dance, and everyone fasts on this day.

Many festivals begin with a fast before a day of feasting and celebration. During Diwali or the Hindu Feast of Lights, everyone fasts on the third day in honour of the goddess Lakshmi before celebrating the main day of the festival.

The festival commemorating the birth of Krishna, one of the most important gods, begins with a day of fasting which ends at midnight, the time when Krishna is supposed to have been born.

THE FOUR DAYS OF NYUNGNE

On the first day, offerings are made to the local gods. On the second day, everyone gathers in the temple for prayers and recitations.

The fast begins after the midday meal on the second day and lasts until the morning of the fourth day. The ritual ends with an evening feast to celebrate the merit that everyone has gained.

Hindu women fast regularly for the good of their husbands, as a sign that they share his fortunes in life. At one time, Hindu women were seen as inferior to their husbands, but today they are on equal terms with men, although they are still expected to seem deferential to their husbands in public. Women can go on pilgrimages, visit temples, fast and make offerings just like the men do.

Feats of Endurance

People sometimes prove their devotion to their beliefs by undergoing feats of endurance which most of us could not tolerate. In many traditional cultures, from North America to the Pacific Islands, devotees will scar or pierce their bodies in honour of the gods. Fire-walkers stride across red-hot coals without burning themselves and Indian fakirs will sit on a bed of nails without feeling any pain.

In one well-documented case, the fakir Haridas spent forty days buried in a sealed chest at a maharajah's palace. Before his

▲ A THOUSAND CUTS

This islander from Polynesia has inserted a needle through his nose and another through his lower lip. In addition he has hung stones from hooks inserted into his chest and arms. This painful ritual forms part of his initiation ceremony into the secret society of manhood.

burial, Haridas fasted for several days and cleaned out his stomach by swallowing a strip of cloth and then bringing it up again. He sealed his nose and ears so that insects could not get in, rolled his tongue back to cover his throat and relaxed until he seemed to be dead. When he was released from the airless coffin forty days later, an hour of massage restored him to full life and intelligence.

Tibetan Buddhist monks are credited with equal feats of endurance. One test of a true adept (master) is for him to meditate semi-naked in the snow, draped in a wet blanket and to dry the blanket with his body heat.

▲ THE RUNNING MONKS OF JAPAN

One sect of Buddhist monks in Japan has a unique way of acquiring of enlightenment. A monk will dedicate himself to run a specific distance (around 32 kilometres) every day for three years. As time goes on, he must carry heavy weights on his daily run. Any monk that completes this gruelling marathon is hailed as a Bodhisattva (a saint who has achieved enlightenment).

·Artists of the World·

A rt and religion have been linked for thousands of years. The first paintings produced by people, on the walls of caves, were probably connected with religious rituals, and the art left to us by the ancient civilizations is almost all religious. Paintings in tombs and temples, and statues of gods and goddesses give us great insight into the lives of the peoples and also about the religions they followed.

In Europe in the Middle Ages and afterwards, painters and sculptors were mostly supported by the Church who commissioned them to produce works of art for the grand cathedrals and churches that were being built. It was not until wealthy Italian princes, bankers and merchants began to sponsor artists during the Renaissance that they could express themselves more freely. Even then, artists continued to take commissions for decorating religious buildings, and the theme of many Renaissance paintings is religious.

ART AND THE SPIRIT

Works of art from all over the world demonstrate how art and religion have been connected throughout history.

The same was true of the other arts. Music probably began as a part of religious rituals to summon gods, and has continued to play an important part in religion ever since.

When people began to write, the first stories set down were legends about the gods. The earliest surviving known story is the Sumerian *Epic of Gilgamesh*, which tells the story of a legendary king of Erech in Mesopotamia, who was two-thirds god and one-third man, and of his search for immortality after the death of his best friend, the wild man Enkiddu. It was probably first written down in about 2100 BC, but the story is much older than that.

THE TAJ MAHAL, *the magnificent seventeenth-century tomb which the Mogul emperor Shah Jehan built for his wife, Mumtaz-i-Mahal, has gardens which are laid out as an Islamic symbol of paradise.*

This and the African mask showing the face of a spirit, the labyrinth indicating the one way towards God, and the icon of a Christian saint all show how art can lead us into other worlds.

In Closer Touch

All over the world, there are people who claim that they can communicate closely with gods and spirits. The people with special powers may be the shamans of traditional religions who perform rituals in masks and costumes during which they seem to become the spirit they are calling upon.

They may be fortune-tellers who gaze into a crystal ball or read tarot cards to tell the future, or mediums who can call on spirits who then occupy the medium's body while he or she is in a trance.

Whether these rituals are religious or not, they are always strange and mysterious. The techniques used are often a closely guarded secret. The person usually dresses in some unusual way to set him or her apart from the crowd. Very often, he or she will perform some sort of ritual that brings on a trance. This may be done by chanting sounds, words or verses, by leaping around in a wild dance, or by seeming to concentrate the mind and depart from the everyday world, sometimes with a lot of strange and noisy breathing.

Whatever technique is used, the person may go into a frenzy as the tension builds up. Perhaps the chanting becomes louder or the music grows faster and wilder. In parts of Asia, a shaman will whirl himself into a trance and reach a stage of frenzy which is a bit like the medieval dance manias in Europe.

Dancers on the island of Bali in Indonesia work themselves into a frenzied trance, pressing sharp daggers called 'krisses' towards their chests. The mystique surrounding this type of ritual makes onlookers a little afraid of it and therefore less likely to try to find out the secrets.

RELIGIOUS CEREMONIES OFTEN *involve saying, chanting or singing set words. If the words are chanted, they seem particularly spiritual and mysterious. Chanting helps people to achieve a trance-like state which excludes all other thoughts.*

The world of spirits is at the heart of all traditional religions, but people from all over the world have a fear of ghosts and spirits. Most people would rather leave the spirits well alone and not try to communicate with them at all. A graveyard can be a creepy place at night, and ghosts, skeletons and the like are the basis of many a horror story.

So it is not surprising that people from traditional societies who believe that they are surrounded by evil spirits are terrified of upsetting them. Keeping the evil spirits at bay is part of nearly every ritual, particularly those concerned with rites of passage.

In all religions, music and chanting are used to heighten the mood of the worshippers and emphasize the importance of the text. The Islamic call to prayer chanted by the muezzin from the minaret of the mosque sounds very dramatic as it rings out across the town: 'God is most great. I testify that there is no god but Allah. I testify that Muhammad is God's Prophet. Come to prayer, come to security. God is most great.'

Hindus use music and chanting in many ways. One of the most well known is the chanting of the sacred syllable 'AUM' or 'OM'. The three sounds which make up this syllable symbolize Brahma (A), Vishnu (U) and Shiva (M). This is just one example of a chant which has great meaning though there are no words. It illustrates the power of chanting and sacred music in religious rituals, whether they are designed to calm people, whip them into a frenzy or conjure up or banish spirits.

Shamans

The shaman is the central person in many traditional religions. His supernatural powers give him great influence over people in the community, and he may be the chief as well as the priest and medicine man.

The Inuit of the Arctic coast live in a bleak cold world of snow and icy seas. They believe that they are surrounded by spirits who control every aspect of their environment. The Inuit traditionally live by hunting animals such as seals and bears. They believe that when they kill another living thing they are held responsible for releasing its soul, and this must be done with the proper ritual.

The Inuit goddess Sedna, who is half human and half fish, lives in a great cave under the sea and releases sea animals for the hunters to catch. If they do not observe certain rituals and treat their prey with respect, or if they break one of the many taboos surrounding hunting, Sedna will be angry and will hold back the animals. Sedna is the most powerful goddess, but the Inuit believe that each land animal also has a spirit who guards it and decides whether or not to release it to the hunters, depending on their behaviour on previous kills.

At the centre of all this ritual is the 'angakut' or shaman, who helps the people keep the right balance between the need to find food and the need to keep the spirits happy. The shaman acts as a go-between for the hunters. If there is a shortage of animals to hunt, the shaman goes into a frenzied trance during which he sends out one of his souls to find out who has broken a taboo and angered the spirits.

A person becomes a shaman because he or she has had a vision or dream which tells him that he or she has special powers. (It is fairly unusual for women to become shamans.) When the decision has been made, the novice learns from a shaman who knows the secrets of the tribe's magic. The Inuit shaman must be able to imagine the inside of his body and name all the bones in his skeleton. He must also spend a time alone, fasting and suffering from the cold. If he is worthy to become a shaman, this endurance test should bring him visions and a guiding spirit who will help him on his quest through the spirit world.

When the new shaman comes out of his retreat and returns to his people, he can begin to act as their link between life and spirits. He will do this by performing ceremonies at which drums and chanting help to send him into a trance. Thus his 'free soul' is released to seek for the knowledge the people need to survive.

The shaman's success or failure depends on the results of these quests. If he sends his soul out to find the reason for a lack of animals to hunt, and the animals then begin to appear again, everyone will applaud his special powers. But if the animals still stay away, he has failed. In the same way, he is expected to diagnose diseases and to forecast the weather and make predictions about good times to travel or go hunting.

THE YAKUT PEOPLE *of Siberia believe that the shaman keeps his soul in the body of an animal which is hidden away. Once a year, when the snows are melting, the animals come out of their hiding places, but only the shamans can see them. The strongest shamans are the ones whose souls are kept in powerful animals like black bears and eagles. The weakest keep their souls in dogs.*

Voodoo

In 1492, Columbus discovered an island in the Caribbean which he called Espanola. It was on this island, later called Hispaniola, that the Spanish established their first settlement in the New World. They colonized the eastern side of the island, which they called Santo Domingo and, after some wrangling with the British, French settlers took over the western side. The French part of the island was later known as Haiti. Today, Haiti forms one-third of the island. The rest is the Dominican Republic.

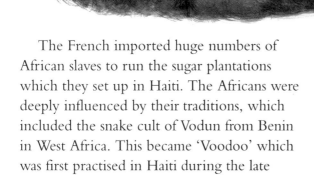

The French imported huge numbers of African slaves to run the sugar plantations which they set up in Haiti. The Africans were deeply influenced by their traditions, which included the snake cult of Vodun from Benin in West Africa. This became 'Voodoo' which was first practised in Haiti during the late seventeenth century, and has now spread to Cuba, Jamaica and Brazil.

Like other traditional religions, Voodoo is based on myths and magic. Worshippers believe that the spirits of the dead can be called up by magical rituals, to either bless or curse the living. Ritual dances are an

sinister cult, particularly because of the way that it has been used in Haiti.

In 1791, the Black slaves, influenced by the French Revolution with its message of equality and freedom, began to revolt against their French masters. At first, the new republican government in France was pleased because many settlers supported the French monarchy. But so many settlers were massacred that the government had to step in to crush the revolt in 1792. The Black leader, Toussaint L'Ouverture, negotiated with the French and finally took over the whole island, making it the world's first Black republic in 1801.

The French attempted to recapture Haiti and bring back slavery which L'Ouverture had abolished. They were finally driven out in 1803, and the new Black leader Jean-Jacques Dessalines proclaimed himself Emperor Jacques I of the republic. A line of self-styled 'emperors' followed him until 1859.

Meanwhile, the children of European and Black parents, known as 'mulattos' in Haiti, were struggling to free themselves from the tyrannical rule of the Blacks. Fighting between the two groups continued throughout the nineteenth century. The Blacks were steeped in the traditions of their Voodoo cult. The mulattos stuck to the French traditions they knew. Constant unrest brought the country into total confusion with deep debts.

The USA occupied Haiti in 1905 and tried to sort out the country's problems, but withdrew in 1934. The dictator François Duvalier, known as Papa Doc, became president, and Haiti became a police state which used Voodoo and a private army, the Tonton Macoutes, to force people to follow its brutal regime. Many of Duvalier's opponents were murdered, supposedly by being given the 'evil eye'. His reign of terror ended with his death in 1971, but his son, known as Baby Doc, carried on ruling in the same way until ousted in 1986. However, survivers of the Tonton Macoutes still terrorize the people.

important part of Voodoo celebrations and ceremonies. A priest or priestess will be present, but the worshippers carry out the dances to the accompaniment of drums. They shuffle back and forth, shaking their bodies, rolling their eyes and chanting strange words. They often get into such a frenzied state that they begin to froth at the mouth. The evil elements of Voodoo make it a

•Oracles and Soothsayers•

An oracle is an answer to a specific questions supplied by the gods or spirits. The oracle can be a person, usually a priest or priestess, who seems to reply in the voice of a god or spirit. There are other types of oracle, such as interpreting the shapes left by tea-leaves in a cup. Oracles have been used for thousands of years, and are the basis of many ancient religions.

The Oracle at Delphi in ancient Greece is one of the most well-known examples, but the Greeks themselves used other forms of oracle. One of these was known as 'incubation'. The person seeking an answer to a question spent the night in the temple, and the answer would come to him in a dream. The oldest oracle shrine in Greece was the Talking Oak of Dodona where priests acted as the voice of Zeus and gave his answers by rustling the boughs or banging on a gong.

In ancient China, 'soothsayers' used oracle bones to foretell future happenings. The soothsayer would ask a question to the spirits by inscribing it on the shell of a tortoise or the leg bone of an ox. A heated bronze point was applied to the bone to make it crack. The soothsayer then 'read' the message in the cracks and gave the spirits' answer. This method was used by the kings of the Shang dynasty, who ruled from 1760 to 1100 BC, the first period of Chinese history of which there is any record. People in China still consult an oracle or fortune-teller about important decisions or happenings in their lives.

The Chinese also believed that dreams foretold the future, as did many of the

ancient civilizations. Dreams were regarded as messages from the gods, rather than the workings of the subconscious mind.

A Roman seer called Artemidorus wrote a work called *The Five Books of the Interpretation of Dreams*, in which he detailed the ways in which ancient peoples worked out what their dreams meant. Some of these methods are still the basis of dream interpretation today.

One story about a dream coming up with an answer to a problem tells of a nineteenth-century professor of Assyrian history who had been trying to decipher writing on two ancient pieces of agate which he believed came from Babylon. He had written his conclusions in a book, but was not happy that he had got it right. Still worrying about the problem, he went to bed and fell into an exhausted sleep. In his dreams, a priest appeared and told him that he was quite wrong about the pieces of agate. The priest told the professor the true story, saying that he himself had cut the pieces from a cylinder used to make offerings. When the professor woke up, he put the pieces together and saw that they had been cut from the same object. He was able to use this evidence to piece them together and decipher them.

In ancient Mesopotamia, oracles foretold the future by studying the livers of sacrificed animals. In Egypt and other Arab countries, people still use the 'zairgeh' or magic square. One of the simplest versions is a grid of small squares, each containing a letter. The person wanting advice first says some verses of the Qur'an. He or she then concentrates hard on the problem and, with closed eyes, sticks a pin or the point of a pencil into the square to choose a letter. The letter which is chosen is then written down and then every eighth letter is added in the order in which they appear on the square. The resulting word is supposed to be the answer to the question.

The same person must not consult the magic square more than once a month.

The Wheel of Fortune is another oracle said to give very accurate predictions. The wheel is made up of segments representing the twelve signs of the zodiac with an arrangement of numbers inside them. The person wanting a prediction should close their eyes and stick a pin firstly into a sign of the zodiac, and then into a number to receive an answer.

SPEAKING IN TONGUES, *that is in an unknown language, is another oracular method. The Bible tells us that after the Holy Ghost descended on the apostles at Pentecost, they spoke in tongues and when they preached in the street, each listener heard their words in their own language, despite the fact that the apostles were speaking in Aramaic.*

Fortune-tellers

Clairvoyants, or fortune-tellers, still use some of the ancient methods of looking into someone's future. An old favourite is crystal-gazing in which people with special clairvoyant powers can stare into a crystal ball and see visions of the future. The ancients probably used a globe made of rock crystal, although crystal balls are more likely to be made of clear glass today. Other things besides crystal itself can have the desired effect. The clairvoyant gazes deep into the ball until he or she sees pictures in it which are said to be brought about by supernatural forces.

Mirrors and pools of clear water have been used in a similar way to the crystal ball in some societies. Every magician of the Middle Ages had a mirror in which he could see visions of the future. 'Specularii' or mirror-diviners, were established in ancient Rome, and mirror divinations play a part in the Shinto religion of Japan. In some parts of the ancient world, people were afraid to look into a pool of water in case they saw anything they would rather not know about. People in ancient India believed that it was bad luck to see

one's reflection in water, while to the ancient Greeks it was an omen of death.

In the Middle Ages, crystal-gazing was usually accompanied by magical ceremonies. Magicians would chant prayers and spells and burn perfumes to help the vision along. Strange herbal concoctions were drunk to help the clairvoyant's powers, and the moon had to be waxing, or becoming fuller, for the crystal-gazing to work.

Another ancient, but still popular method is reading cards, which may be tarot cards or ordinary playing cards. Card diviners believe that Monday and Friday are particularly lucky days for looking into the future. The best time is thought to be early evening on a clear, calm day. If ordinary playing cards are being

used, the diviner deals the cards out face down and asks the person whose fortune is being told to pick thirteen at random. The diviner then spreads out the chosen cards and reads the fortune according to what the cards mean and how they are grouped together.

Tarot cards show mysterious symbols and pictures such as the Juggler, the Falling Tower, the High Priestess, the Hermit and the more sinister Hanged Man, Death and the Devil. As with playing cards, each card has its own meaning. No one is sure how or where tarot cards originated, but one theory is that the designs come from the Sacred Book of Thoth from ancient Egypt. The fortune is told as a result of the way the cards fall when they are laid out in certain formations.

Spiritualism

A 'medium' is someone who can call up the spirits of the dead. One method used is a ritual called a 'seance'. People wanting to call up spirits sit around a table, and the medium goes into a trance. While in the trance, he or she appears to receive messages from spirits, sometimes through one spirit who acts as an interpreter. People around the table can ask the medium to contact the spirits of members of their family or friends and then ask the spirits questions. The medium replies as though the spirits are talking through his or her mouth. Spiritualists have a church network as well.

Dealing with Evil

Sometimes people feel the need to rid themselves or others of evil influences. In some cultures, these are believed to be evil spirits who 'possess' people, or take over their bodies and make them do bad things. In others, the ghosts of the dead are thought to return to haunt the living.

Some ghosts are placid and harmless, while others are trouble-makers and disrupt people's lives. 'Poltergeists' are ghosts which mysteriously throw things around the room and cause other forms of havoc. Ghosts of this type have to be 'exorcized' or got rid of in a special ceremony conducted by a priest.

I n India, all Hindu villages have a specialist who can rid people of evil spirits. If someone is in trouble or has an illness, he or she will first try to cure it by natural remedies. If these fail, however, it may be decided that evil spirits are at work, and depending on the problem, a priest or exorcist will be called in.

The priests, who are known as 'informal priests', are different from the high-caste Brahmans. They are usually of a lower caste and are thought to have a direct link with the god or goddess of the village. Hindus believe that the gods speak to them through the mouths of these priests. The priest conducts a ritual in which he goes into a trance and speaks as the voice of the god, telling the villager what the problem is. This may be that the god is angry for some reason and wants an offering. The priest also prescribes a remedy for the problem, which usually involves carrying out a sequence of rituals to appease the god or goddess.

Exorcists deal with people who are possessed by an evil spirit or a ghost. To Hindus, a ghost is the spirit of someone who died a sudden or unnatural death. The rites at the funeral did not lay the person to rest effectively, and so the ghost remains on Earth, haunting others. The most frightening ghosts are women who died in childbirth or without having children.

When an exorcist is called to a possessed person, he carries out some rituals and asks

the ghost to leave. The ghost will tell the exorcist the terms for leaving, such as requiring offerings, and an agreement will be reached. The exorcist goes through more rituals to persuade the ghost to come out, and then traps it in some object, which he takes away to place the ghost elsewhere.

The Vikings believed that a warrior who died in his bed could come back as an evil ghost. The only way to lay such a ghost was to kill it in hand-to-hand combat because then the dead man would qualify for Valhalla. To prevent such hauntings, corpses were sometimes staked through the heart to stop them 'walking'. This is the same method that was later used to avert potential vampires.

Christians believe that ghosts haunt places rather than people, and a priest may be called in to exorcize a poltergeist from a house where it is causing a nuisance. Ghosts are thought to be the spirits of people who have died violent or unnatural deaths, so their identity can often be traced or guessed at. The belief is that the soul of the dead person cannot rest in peace because of the manner of its death. The priest performs a short service aimed at helping the troubled soul to find peace and therefore leave the living alone.

Witches

People have always been afraid of witches because of their association with the devil and evil. During the Dark Ages in Europe, people assumed that any strange happenings were caused by supernatural powers and many women who simply made herbal medicines were accused of practising magic. Witch hunts were carried out throughout the Middle Ages, and women who were thought to be witches were often tortured before being burned at the stake.

In parts of Spain, a ritual for expelling witches was carried out every Friday night in March, the month when witches were thought to roam. The church bells were rung, and everyone rushed through the streets shouting, 'March is come', in an effort to send the witches away.

In central Europe, the favourite night for expelling witches was Walpurgis Night, on the eve of May Day. People ran through the town brandishing burning bundles of twigs and banging pots and pans to make as much noise as possible. Every bell in the town rang out, as everyone screamed 'Witch, flee, flee from here, or it will go ill with thee.' Then they ran around the houses to smoke out the witches and drive them away.

Another time for driving out witches was the week between Christmas and New Year. In some parts of Europe, pine-wood fires were kept burning during this time, so that the strong smoke would drive witches and evil spirits away. Another custom was 'shooting the witches', when young men fired guns into the air to frighten them away.

People used to carry protective charms to ward off the effects of witchcraft. A piece of knotted string was thought to keep witches and wizards away and also to protect a person from death. In 1572, a woman in Scotland was about to be burned alive because she was

THE PRE-CHRISTIAN FESTIVAL of Hallowe'en is still a traditional 'witches' night'. People used to believe that witches were up to their worst mischief on this night, speeding through the air on broomsticks or galloping along on cats turned into black horses for the occasion. Witch hunts were carried out throughout the Middle Ages, and many women who were thought to be witches were often tortured before being burned at the stake or drowned.

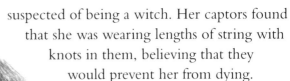
suspected of being a witch. Her captors found that she was wearing lengths of string with knots in them, believing that they would prevent her from dying.

When the strings were taken away from her, she said 'Now I have no hope of myself', knowing that her fate was sealed.

People also thought that a witch's power was kept in her hair. In France, anyone who was suspected of witchcraft had their head shaved before being tortured, because it was felt the torture would have no effect if the witch still had her hair. Similarly, it was felt that a witch could not be burned to death unless all her hair had been shaved off. There are stories of suspected witches who put up with incredible pain during torture until cutting off their hair made them give in and confess their guilt.

In India, men or women who were suspected of witchcraft were beaten by the crowd, their hair was shaved off and hung up on a tree in a public place and their front teeth were knocked out to prevent them from muttering spells. In one part of India, a woman thought to be a witch was hung upside down from a tree and had pepper put into her eyes. If that failed to make her confess, a lock of her hair was cut off and buried in the ground to break her powers.

However, not all witches are wicked, contrary to fairy tales! There are many people around the world today who call themselves white witches and who follow a religion known as Wicca. This involves both worship of a Goddess and rituals of traditional witchcraft but these are used to achieve good, not evil.

·Witch Hunts in Africa·

The religions of traditional cultures in Africa has always been heavily tied up with magic, and there is a strong belief in witchcraft. Witch-finding is an important activity which involves rituals by a medicine man or diviner. If someone suspects that a member of the community is a witch, he approaches the medicine man or diviner and outlines his suspicions. The rituals which are carried out are designed to protect people from the suspected witch, and also to persuade the witch to stop his or her activities.

IN KENYA AND *Tanzania, there are whole villages of women who have been expelled from their homes because they have been accused of witchcraft. Often this is a made-up charge so that a husband can marry a younger wife, or a son obtain his mother's property.*

In central Africa, there are groups of people who specialize in hunting witches. They travel from place to place conducting rituals designed to clear whole communities of any witches by making them confess and so lose their powers.

The Azande tribe who live in the Sudan, Zaire and the Central African Republic believe that the things they see in their dreams are real events. Nice dreams foretell good fortune, but unpleasant dreams are the result of someone in the community practising witchcraft. To the Azande, anything bad that happens is a result of witches getting up to mischief, and death

is a sure sign of witchcraft. When someone is asleep, the Azande say, the soul leaves the body and wanders around.

Witches also release their souls to roam about at night. A bad dream is the result of the person's soul meeting up with the soul of a witch. A person who has had a bad dream has to go straight to a diviner who tries to find out who the witch is by a process of rituals and questions. When the witch has been identified, he or she is then persuaded to stop the witchcraft.

A bizarre way of finding out if someone is

MANY TRADITIONAL CULTURES *in Africa believe that all illnesses are caused by witchcraft. It has been known for people to die of a minor illness because they believe that they have been bewitched.*

a witch is practised in Kenya. A frog is put into the accused person's mouth. If it refuses to go down his throat, the person is innocent, but if the person swallows the frog, he is judged to be guilty.

In West Africa, witches and wizards are believed to have animal companions known as 'familiars' which give them their power. Wizards are said to choose powerful animals such as leopards and panthers and go through a ritual in which they take blood from the animal's ear and inject some of their own blood into the animal. In this way, the wizard

takes on the strength of the animal, and if the animal dies, the wizard dies too. The dreaded leopard men of Kenya do this as well.

Witches are thought to choose smaller animals such as vultures, owls and poisonous snakes as their familiars. These animals are always wild and usually dangerous. They are said to obey every command from their 'blood brother', and so can be used to injure or kill enemies. It is supposed to be impossible to kill the wizard or witch while his or her familiar is alive. The only way to get rid of the person is to kill the animal.

Superstitions

People all over the world have superstitions about what brings good and bad luck and protection from evil influences. One of the most popular methods of protection is carrying a mascot. The word 'mascot' comes from the French word 'masco' which means sorcerer. The mascot is supposed to provide the sorcery or magic needed to bring good luck and fend off evil.

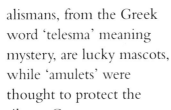

T alismans, from the Greek word 'telesma' meaning mystery, are lucky mascots, while 'amulets' were thought to protect the wearer from the evil eye. Grotesque objects were often chosen as amulets so that the evil eye would look away in disgust. Alternatively the amulets could be charms which were worn in the clothing. All sorts of talismans were used to bring success in love, to cure disease, to make the person rich or to ensure victory in battle. They were normally symbols carved on to bone, wood or stone.

In ancient Egypt, cats were often carved on to amulets because they were regarded as particularly sacred and therefore lucky. In medieval Europe, on the other hand, cats were associated with witches, and were thought unlucky.

Beads were lucky symbols in ancient times. 'Eye beads', thought to represent the eye of the gods, were carried around to ward off danger and to bring women luck in their love affairs.

Another universal symbol of luck is the fish. In ancient Egypt, it represented Hathor,

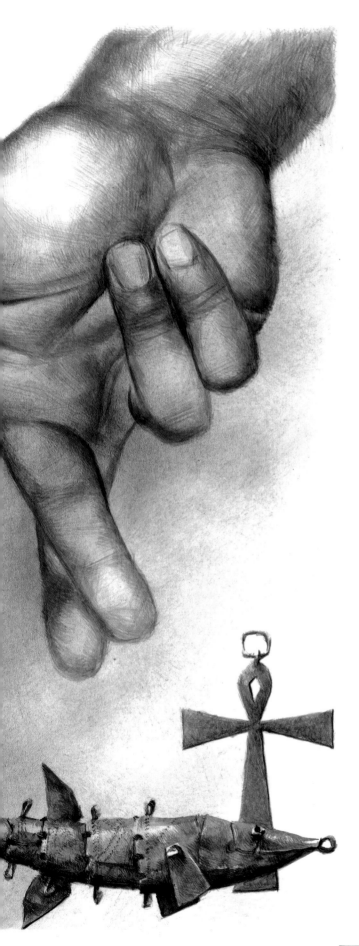

the cow-headed goddess, who controlled the flooding of the Nile. Early Christians adopted the fish as a symbol of Jesus, while in Japan it is a sign of endurance and courage.

The horseshoe is one of the best-known lucky symbols which is still used today. It has been nailed on to the doors of houses since the days of the Greeks. Roman women wore crescent symbols on their shoes to protect them from madness and hysteria brought on by the Moon. The horseshoe gradually took on the same significance as the crescent because of its similar shape.

Omens

Throughout history, people have seen dark or lucky omens in things which have happened. When William of Normandy first set foot on English soil before the Battle of Hastings in 1066, he stumbled and fell flat on his face. His army saw this as an omen that they would lose the battle. But the duke, with great presence of mind, said 'Thus I seize this land with both my hands', turning his accident into a sign of good fortune. He was right, of course, but his soldiers must have been worried until the battle was safely won.

Animals are often seen as omens of good or bad luck. Having a black cat cross your path is a confusing omen. Some people say it is lucky and others that it is unlucky. But did you know that it is bad luck to meet a donkey coming in the opposite direction? Meeting a goat brings wealth, and a piebald horse is a lucky sign, so long as you do not see its tail first. It is also good luck to meet a flock of sheep if you are on a journey.

If you meet a squirrel you will be happy, but not if you meet a weasel. Hardly surprisingly, the black rat is one of the worst things you can see. If your belongings are gnawed by rats, put off doing anything you had planned as it will certainly go wrong.

Theatrical Fears

People all over the world also have superstitions which involve rituals that have to be carried out to avoid misfortune.

Actors are among the most superstitious people, with a whole string of things that are certain to make the show go wrong. Whistling in the dressing room is very bad luck. If anyone does this, he or she must go out of the room, turn around three times and then knock for permission to come back in.

The number thirteen is thought to be unlucky by actors, as by many other people, and so is the colour green. Real flowers should never be used on stage, and a costume which includes peacock feathers is disastrous.

If an actor or actress notices a loose thread on someone's clothes, this can bring good luck, provided the actor pulls off the thread, passes it around his head three times and tucks it down the neck of his clothes. This ritual should ensure a new contract for work!

You should never wish an actor good luck as this will anger the gods. The traditional good luck saying is 'Break a leg!' Such misfortune could really happen to an actor in Shakespeare's play *Macbeth*, which is so unlucky that no one may even mention it by name – it is usually called 'the Scottish play'. The reason is that the witches' song is supposed to call up evil spirits who will find some way of inflicting harm on the actors.

The Evil Eye

Many old superstitions concern the evil eye and its association with witchcraft. People whose eyes were too close together or set deep in their head, or who squinted, were often accused of having the evil eye and could be put to death on this evidence alone. Country people used to believe that the evil eye looking on them could bring suffering to their families or animals, so if someone fell ill after a look from an old woman with deep-set eyes, this was enough to seal the old woman's fate. Making the sign of the cross was thought to guard against the evil eye, as was spitting three times into the witch's eyes.

Although it is supposed to be lucky to meet a goat, this animal is also linked with the devil in some societies. The devil was thought to take on the form of a goat when he wanted to travel around unnoticed, yet other people think that hair from a goat's beard is an amulet against the devil.

GOOD LUCK OR bad luck? Many people believe that thirteen is an unlucky number and refuse to sit down if there are thirteen at table. The Savoy Hotel in London keeps a stuffed black cat especially to act as the fourteenth person at table if this should occur.

One of the most well-known superstitions is that it is bad luck to walk under a ladder, and many people think that the simple reason is the danger of getting a pot of paint or bucket of water on your head. But this is in fact an old Christian superstition which is also linked with the devil. A ladder leaning against a wall forms a triangle which was a symbol of the Holy Trinity: Father, Son and Holy Ghost. To walk through this triangle was said to show that you had sympathy with the devil. However, people who do walk under a ladder can make things right by keeping their fingers crossed until they meet a dog.

Shoes are linked with many old superstitions. Putting your shoes on the wrong feet is said to bring bad luck. This superstition goes back to Emperor Augustus who came close to being assassinated after putting his sandals on the wrong feet. If you buy new shoes, never put them on the table or you may bring bad luck to the whole family. But if you do not give at least one pair of new shoes as a present during your life, you will go barefoot in the next world. In the Far East, many people believe that if you leave a pair of shoes lying upside down, you will quarrel with someone that day.

Find Out Some More

Books to Read

The Christian Church by Thomas Sikes Hichens (Oxford University Press, 1971)

The Christian World by Alan Brown (Simon and Schuster, 1984)

Festivals in World Religion edited by Alana Brown (Longman, 1986)

Founders of Religions by Tony D. Triggs (Wayland, 1981)

Gods and Pharaohs from Egyptian Mythology by Geraldine Harris (Peter Lowe, 1982)

Hinduism by Madhu Bazaz Waugu (Facts on File, 1991)

Islam by Matthew S. Gordon (Facts on File, 1991)

Judaism by Myer Domnitz (Wayland, 1986)

Judaism by Martha Morrison and Stephen F. Brown (Facts on File, 1991)

Lands of the Bible, The in the MYSTERIOUS PLACES series by Robert Ingpen & Jacqueline Dineen (Dragon's World, 1992)

Magical East, The in the MYSTERIOUS PLACES series by Robert Ingpen & Michael Pollard (Dragon's World, 1992)

Master Builders, The in the MYSTERIOUS PLACES series by Robert Ingpen & Michael Pollard (Dragon's World, 1992)

Mediterranean, The in the MYSTERIOUS PLACES series by Robert Ingpen & Jacqueline Dineen (Dragon's World, 1992)

Mesopotamian Myths by I. McCall (British Museum Publications, 1990)

Religions of the World by Lynn Underwood (Belitha Press, 1991)

Religious Services by Jon Mayled (Wayland, 1986)

Stories from the Sikh World by Rani and Jugnu Singh (Macdonald, 1987)

Taoism by Paula R. Hartz (Facts on File, 1993)

For Older Readers

You might like to try some of these books to find out more background information about some of the peoples in this book.

The Atlas of the Ancient World by Margaret Oliphant (Marshall Editions, 1992)

The Atlas of Early Man by Jacquetta Hawkes (Macmillan, 1976)

The Golden Bough (A History of Myth and Religion) by Sir James Frazer (Chancellor Press, 1994)

Kingdoms of Gold, Kingdoms of Jade (*The Americas before Columbus*) by Brian M. Fagan (Thames and Hudson, 1991)

Viking Age England by Julian D. Richards (Batsford, 1991)

World Faiths by S.A. Nigosian (St Martin's Press, New York, 1994)

World Mythology, general editor Roy Willis (Duncan Baird Publishers, 1993)

Places to Visit

Many museums have exhibits from the ancient world and events in history. Visit your local museum, or ask at your local library for suggestions where to see ethnic collections.

- Most religions welcome interested inquirers. But please remember that some religious ceremonies, like marriages and funerals, have intense personal meaning to those involved. Don't push in where you are unwelcome.

- Ask your teacher if he or she could arrange a visit to the local synagogue or mosque. It is best to make an official visit as you don't want to upset people by not behaving suitably in their holy place.

- Speak to The Sikh Missionary Society, 10 Featherstone Road, Southall, Middlesex UB2 5AA about visiting a gurdwara.

Index